THE ROUGH GUIDE TO

Walks
in London
and
southeast
England

Rough Guides online

www.roughguides.com

Rough Guide credits

Text editor: Gavin Thomas
Series editor: Mark Ellingham
Production: Katie Pringle, John McKay

Cover credits

Main front photograph: Long Man, Wilmington © Pictures of
Britain/Anthony Cook
Lower left front cover photo: Blackthorn hedge © Helena Smith
Lower middle front cover photo: Little Venice, London © Getty
Lower right front cover photo: Green Man, The Parkland Way
© Helena Smith
Top back cover photo: The Pilgrims' Way © Helena Smith
Lower back cover photo: Saxon church, Bosham © Helena Smith

Publishing information

This edition published August 2003 by Rough Guides Ltd,
80 Strand, London WC2R 0RL

Distributed by the Penguin Group

Penguin Books Ltd, 80 Strand, London WC2R 0RL
Penguin Putnam, Inc., 375 Hudson Street, New York 10014, USA
Penguin Books Australia Ltd, 487 Maroondah Highway,
PO Box 257, Ringwood, Victoria 3134, Australia
Penguin Books Canada Ltd, 10 Alcorn Avenue, Toronto,
Ontario M4V 1E4, Canada
Penguin Books (NZ) Ltd, 182–190 Wairau Road, Auckland 10, New
Zealand

Printed in Italy by LegoPrint S.p.A

© Rough Guides
288pp, includes index
A catalogue record for this book is available from the British Library.

ISBN 1-85828-938-6

THE ROUGH GUIDE TO

Walks in London and southeast England

by Judith Bamber
and Helena Smith

ROUGH
GUIDES

Acknowledgements

Helena: Sincere thanks to editor Gavin, whose intelligent contributions to the tone and content of this book have been invaluable. Also to Kate for editorial support; Maxine, Katie and the Map Studio, Romsey, Hants, for creating the maps; Katie P. for skilled typesetting; Louise for the cover; Susannah Wight for proofreading; and Richard and Niki for marketing ideas. Thanks too to the National Trust; to Merrell for the shoes; and to Pevsner guides for a fine collection of books. An enormous thank you to the people who came walking with me and provided encouragement and good cheer: Matt McC.; David & Nicky; Betty, Mike & Ruth Wooldridge; Rachael (Goz); Sara; Lisa & Andy; Lorna & Andy; and Ellen. I am also very grateful to ace walk-testers Clifton, Sally, Philippa, Ruth & Dylan, Lucy & Luca, Katie L-J., Jules, Richard (again!), Dave W., Katie Westlake, Jessica Lovejoy, Kate Smith, Dave Reed and Ed Freeman. Special thanks and love, for their wonderful companionship and support, to my brother Dan & (Lady) Sarah, my parents Grahame & Angela, and my friend Markie.

Judith: Thanks to George, Lisa and Sally for company along the way; to Lynda and Bob for reminding me to have faith in myself; and especially to Geoff for support above and beyond. Thanks also to Gavin for his punctilious editing.

Contents

Five of the best: Roman remains

Anderida A still formidable ring of Roman walls, built to keep Saxon pirates at bay. See p.104

Calleva This major Roman settlement escaped subsequent development, and the town walls and amphitheatre remain remarkably intact. See p.163

Fishbourne Palace The finest in-situ mosaic floors in the country. See p.113

North Leigh Roman Villa The scant but evocative remains of a Roman villa, set in a green valley. See p.194

Verulamium The remains of a major Roman trading post, dotted around a park in St Albans. See p.210

example, is at its best in late spring with the rhododendrons and azaleas in full bloom, while the orchards of Kent dazzle with blossom in spring and have a more mellow allure in autumn, when the trees are heavy with fruit. But, in general, any time of year is a good time to do these walks and, in the temperate climate of southern England, you're unlikely to encounter truly wild weather. There are, of course, fewer hours of daylight for winter walks, but the austere beauty of wintry landscapes can hold as much appeal as more verdant summer ones.

The Grand Union Canal

Horsenden Hill and around

Distance and difficulty: 6km; easy.
Train: Piccadilly Line to Alperton (zone 4); return on the Central Line from Greenford (zone 4).
Map: OS Landranger 176: *West London*; OS Explorer 173: *London North*.

This walk follows the quiet and leafy course of the **Grand Union Canal** as it winds through west London. Built in 1801, the canal linked London to the rest of the country's canal system, beginning in Birmingham and terminating at the Paddington basin. The canal brought new industries to the area, and within three generations this formerly agricultural community had been subsumed by the city's western sprawl. Nearby **Perivale**, a hamlet when the canal arrived, still retains a village-like feel.

Following the towpath west from **Alperton**, this walk leads out past Horsenden Farm to **Horsenden Hill**, from whose summit there are superb views across the city and out to the countryside north and west of London. Beyond here, the walk continues west along the canal, past **Perivale Wood** and around the bird-rich wetlands of **Paradise Fields** to finish in nearby **Greenford**. There's nowhere at present to eat along the route (though Horsenden Farm, just below the hill, has plans to open a café in the near future), so this walk is best done as a morning's or afternoon's stroll, or around a **picnic** on the hill.

Getting started

0.3km

From **Alperton tube station**, turn right onto the A4089 (Ealing Road). Cross over the road at the pedestrian crossing, just beyond the station forecourt, then turn right and head straight down to the T-junction with the A4005 (Bridgewater Road). Turn left here and cross the road bridge over the **Grand Union Canal**, on the far side of which steps lead down to the canal. At the bottom of the steps, turn left and then left again onto the towpath and head under the road bridge.

Along the Grand Union Canal

1.7km

Framed by the bridge, dotted with colourful narrow boats and frequented by swans and moorhens, the canal makes a surprisingly tranquil contrast to the road above. After 500m

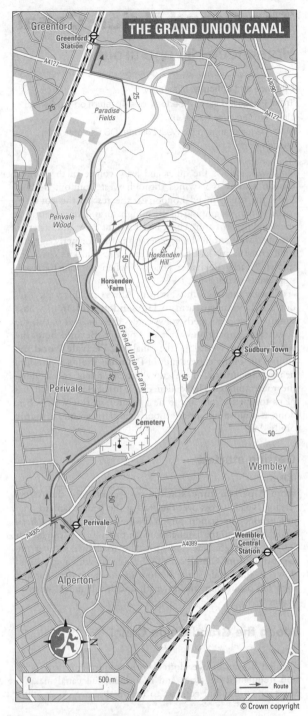

Greenford
Greenford
Station

A4127

A4127

A4080

Paradise
Fields

25

25

25

Perivale
Wood

25

50

Horsenden
Hill

75

Horsenden
Farm

Grand Union Canal

50

Sudbury Town

Perivale

25

50

Cemetery

Wembley

50

Perivale

50

A4005

Wembley
Central
Station

A4089

Alperton

N

0   500 m

→ Route

© Crown copyright

the views begin to open up ahead as you skirt the southern side of Alperton's **cemetery**, opened during World War I and maintained in part by the War Graves Commission (though all you can see from here is the attractive red-brick chapel and a few gravestones), and hilly **Sudbury Golf Course** beyond, with Horsenden Hill rising steeply at its western reaches.

Beneath the hill nestles **Horsenden Farm**. The farm was here long before the canal, but took full advantage of the waterway, becoming a major supplier of hay to the capital (which it exchanged for manure from the city's streets). The farm is now given over to a rowing club and a kids' adventure trail – you can see the wooden sculptures which line the latter, including a giant heron, a tiny narrow boat and flying fish, across the canal – and is a particularly pleasant spot, with willows overhanging the waterside and herons, moorhens and ducks splashing around on the canal itself. At the time of writing, long-term plans to open a **café** in the grounds were still in the pipeline.

Horsenden Hill

2km

Continue along the towpath to the western end of Horsenden Farm, just beyond a metal kissing gate, where you reach a narrow Victorian road bridge and, flanking it, a modern pedestrian bridge, sympathetically designed with imitation wrought-iron railings to harmonize with its older neighbour. Cross the pedestrian bridge, passing the gated entrance to the farm, and follow the pavement round the bend to the left to reach an information board at the foot of **Horsenden Hill**.

Here, a dirt track heads off the pavement and up onto the hill. Heading up a series of rough dirt steps the track emerges in less than 100m onto heath and grass land, rich with wild flowers and butterflies in summer. A solitary oak tree, improbably lolly-pop shaped, stands just to your right; the track leads to your right a few metres before it, heading on up the hillside, back into the trees and up a series of dirt steps to emerge after 300m on the grassy summit. This is a popular spot for kite-flying, with rough-hewn benches, plenty of grassy banks to settle down on to catch the sun, and sweeping views north to Harrow-on-the-Hill, southeast to central London and west out of London as far as the Chilterns.

To continue the walk, head down at the northwestern corner of the hilltop, through heath land to **Horsenden Lane**, a quiet thoroughfare which borders fields to the west and has a pleasantly out-of-town feel. Bear left on the path beside it and head downhill to return to the bridge you crossed earlier, over the canal just before Horsenden Farm.

On to Greenford

2km

Turn left at the towpath, head under the bridge and continue west, past **Perivale Wood**. This 27-acre nature reserve protects a patch of ancient oak woodland and is closed to the public except on the first Sunday of May, when the carpets of bluebells for which the woods are renowned are in full bloom. You can, however, see a bit of the wood from the towpath.

To your right, there are good views back to Horsenden Hill. Some 300m beyond Perivale Wood you'll come to a footbridge over the canal. Turn off the towpath here and take the path that leads south, away from the canal and the footbridge and around the edge of **Paradise Fields** wetlands. Occupying two man-made lagoons on former industrial land, the wetlands were established in the late 1990s; they already look well established and attract water birds, including sandpipers and lapwings. The path skirts Paradise Fields for about 500m before reaching steps up to the A4127 (Greenford Road).

Head up here and cross to the far side of the road, following the signs for Greenford underground station: go left and down to the traffic lights just before the bridge under the railway, then right along Rockware Avenue. At the T-junction, 200m further on, turn left onto Oldfield Lane and head under the rail bridge, on the opposite side of which is **Greenford station**.

The Thames Towpath

Kew to Richmond

Distance and difficulty: 7km; easy.
Train: District Line or overground train to Kew Gardens (zone 6).
Map: OS Landranger 176: *West London*; OS Explorer 161: *London South*.

Starting in **Kew**, this gentle stroll follows the **Thames Towpath** past **Kew Botanical Gardens** and the adjacent **Old Deer Park** to **Richmond Riverfront**, where the *Tide Tables Café* makes a good spot for **lunch**. En route, the walk passes the former royal residence of **Kew Palace**, historic **Syon House** and the **King's Observatory**, site of the original meridian line, as well as parts of the beautiful Kew Gardens. All these sites testify to the area's royal connections: from the Plantagenets to the Hanovarians, royal households periodically decamped here to escape the bustle of London. The royal estates at Kew, eight acres of which had been made into a Royal Botanical Gardens, were passed to the state following the death of George III in 1820. Greatly expanded in

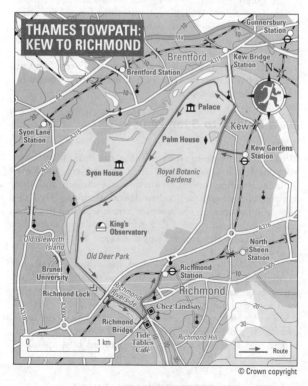

© Crown copyright

the following years, Kew Botanical Gardens today covers some three hundred acres and is a world leader in botanical research as well as one of the capital's most beautiful parks.

Getting started

1.5km

The walk begins at Station Parade, outside the main ticket hall of **Kew Gardens station**. Both tube and overground services from central London deposit you on the opposite side of the tracks. To reach Station Parade, go through the small ticket barrier off this platform, out onto Burlington Avenue, then turn right and head under the subway.

Outside the main ticket hall, two roads lead from the station forecourt: take the one to the left, cross Sandycombe Road at the zebra crossing and continue straight ahead along **Lichfield Road**, following the signs for Kew Gardens. At the end of Lichfield Road you reach **Kew Road** (you'll see the Victoria Gate entrance to Kew Gardens on the opposite side). Cross Kew Road at the pedestrian crossing, turn right and continue for 750m, walking past the gardens' high red-brick boundary wall which flanks the road. Bear left just beyond the northeastern corner of the gardens onto **Kew Green**, a quiet road that runs around the green of the same name.

The green, flanked by Georgian town houses, stands in front of the ornate wrought-iron **gates** that formed the original main entrance to the royal estates at Kew. Cross the green via the path that begins in front of St Anne's Church, just beyond the turn-off from Kew Road. On the far side of the green, head straight ahead down narrow **Ferry Lane**, at the end of which is the Thames and the **Thames towpath**. Head left along the towpath.

Kew Palace to Syon House

1.5km

Within 100m of joining the towpath, views begin to open up to your left into Kew Gardens, revealing elegant **Kew Palace**, standing amidst its ornamental gardens and, just beyond, glimpses of the gardens' **Rhododendron Dell** (in bloom in late spring). The towpath here is separated from the gardens by a small water-filled ditch, which runs along the full length of the former royal estates, all the way to Richmond Lock.

Some 750m beyond Kew Palace, the white, crenellated facade of **Syon House** comes into view through a break in the trees on the opposite bank of the river. Originally the site of a medieval abbey, Syon was dissolved by Henry VIII in 1539 and rebuilt eight years later as a private house. The interiors were remodelled in the eighteenth century by Robert Adam and the 200-acre estate landscaped by Capability Brown. On the Kew side of the river, the aptly named

Sir Joseph Banks at Kew

The first botanical gardens in Kew, covering a modest eight acres, were established by Augusta, the mother of George III, but it wasn't until after her death and George III's acquisition of the Kew estate in 1772 that the botanical gardens began to develop into a world-famous establishment. The key to the gardens' growth was the appointment of **Sir Joseph Banks**, explorer and naturalist, as director of the gardens. Banks had accompanied Captain James Cook on his round-the-world voyage on HMS *Endeavour* four years earlier, collecting a great number of exotic plants, and Banks' vivid descriptions of the trip and of the plants he had gathered sparked enormous interest across Europe, encouraging a generation of botanical collectors to set out around the world and discover new plant species, which were brought back to Kew for classification.

Following George's death in 1820, the gardens were handed over to the state. They were greatly expanded throughout the remainder of the nineteenth century, as well as being extensively landscaped this centred on Decimus Burton's **Palm House**, which was added in 1848. The layout established then survives almost unchanged today, while Kew continues to be a world leader in botanical research – as well as one of London's most beautiful recreation spaces.

Syon Vista, a long, avenue-like clearing, offers views over the Syon estate from Kew's famous **Palm House**, a vast, wrought-iron greenhouse designed by Decimus Burton in 1848 – you might just catch a glimpse of it from the towpath.

The Old Deer Park and King's Obervatory

1.75km

Continue past the small drawbridge that marks the old Isleworth Ferry Gate entrance to the gardens; after 250m you reach the boundary between Kew Gardens and the **Old Deer Park**, which together with the Botanical Gardens formed part of the royal estate of Kew. By 1837, this southern half of the estate had been leased out as pastureland; most of it has now been turned into a golf course and a recreation ground.

Past here, the ditch separating the towpath from the park widens and the river bends round to the south, passing the long island of **Old Isleworth**. Just a few metres beyond the northern end of the island, a stone and steel marker to the left of the towpath marks the position of the old meridian line, which also ran through the stone obelisk on the far side of the moat, just inside the Old Deer Park and the building beyond – the **King's Observatory**. (The official meridian line was only moved from here to Greenwich in the nineteenth century.) The observatory itself was built for George III to observe the transit of Venus in 1769; it later housed his collection of clocks and scientific instruments and was used as a scientific academy for his sons. It's now been turned into offices, but the astronomical dome and its telescopes are still in working order and a small museum has been created in one of the side buildings (open by written request to the Richmond Astronomical Society).

Into Richmond

2.25km

Beyond Old Isleworth island, the fine red-brick Georgian buildings of **Brunel University**'s Twickenham Campus can be seen on the far bank of the river, while ahead, roughly 500m further along the towpath, the ornate wrought-iron footbridge over **Richmond Lock** comes into view. The loose gravel of the towpath gives way to sealed pavements at Richmond Lock as you approach Richmond's riverfront, passing under busy Twickenham Road and then the railway before coming out on well-to-do Cholmondeley Walk, which in turn leads onto **Richmond Riverside**, with its formal landscaping, ersatz Georgian architecture and wealth of cafés, pubs and restaurants.

Tide Tables Café, in the arches below Richmond Bridge, serves hot and cold snacks and has outdoor seating on a garden terrace. For something more substantial, head up onto Richmond Bridge and right at the roundabout to Hill Rise, where *Chez Lindsay* (at no. 11) serves sweet and savoury crepes and has a good-value fixed-price lunch deal; the tables at the back have great views down to the river.

To get to the station, head up the steps at *Tide Tables Café* to reach Richmond Bridge. Turn left onto Richmond Bridge Street, then left at the roundabout onto the main road through town (known variously as Hill Street, George Street and The Quadrant) and follow this for 200m to reach **Richmond station**.

The Thames Towpath

Richmond to Hampton Court Palace

Distance and difficulty: 13–15km; easy–moderate.
Train: District Line tube or overground train from Waterloo to
Richmond (zone 4); return by overground train from Hampton
Court or Teddington (both zone 6) to Waterloo.
Map: OS Landranger 176: *West London*; OS Explorer 161:
London South.

This leafy riverside walk begins in urbane **Richmond** and
then heads upriver along the **Thames Towpath**, through
some of Greater London's most bucolic landscapes. Passing
meadow and woodland, you come to two fine country
estates: creamy-white **Marble Hill**, on the far bank of the
river; and red-brick **Ham House**, on the river's near side.
The *Orangery* tearoom at Ham House is a good spot for
lunch. Beyond Ham, the route passes **Eel Pie Island** and
more meadows before reaching **Kingston-upon-Thames**,
where you cross the river to reach the northern boundary of
Hampton Court Park. There are great views into the park
from the towpath here, which flanks the eastern boundary of
the estate. The walk ends in the attractive village of **Molesey**,
at the main entrance to **Hampton Court Palace**.

Getting started

1km

From **Richmond station**, turn left onto Richmond's main
street, The Quadrant. Follow the road (which subsequently
changes its name to George Street, then Hill Street) for
roughly 500m until the road bends to the left. Turn right
here along Whitaker Walk, which runs past the near side of
the town hall down to **Richmond Riverside**. The riverside
was pedestrianized and terraced in the late 1980s, and this
and the fake Georgian buildings that flank it make the whole
place feel a bit like a stage set. It's a busy spot, even so, with
plenty of teashops, restaurants and ice-cream sellers to cater
to the swarms of people who sit out here on sunny summer
days.

Marble Hill House

2km

Turn left on the Thames Towpath and head under
Richmond Bridge – built in 1777, this elegant five-arch
span of Purbeck stone is London's oldest extant bridge –

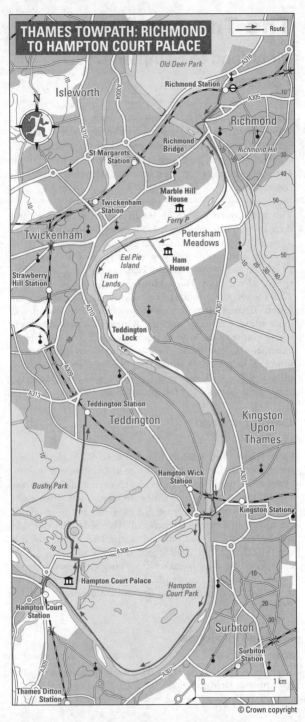

THAMES TOWPATH: RICHMOND TO HAMPTON COURT PALACE

→ Route

Old Deer Park

Richmond Station

A316

A305

Isleworth

A3004

Richmond

A310

St Margarets Station

Richmond Bridge

Richmond Hill

Twickenham Station

Marble Hill House

Ferry P

Petersham Meadows

Twickenham

Eel Pie Island

Ham House

Strawberry Hill Station

Ham Lands

A310

A307

Teddington Lock

A308

A313

Teddington Station

Teddington

Kingston Upon Thames

Bushy Park

Hampton Wick Station

A307

Kingston Station

Hampton Court Palace

Hampton Court Park

Hampton Court Station

A308

Surbiton

A309

Surbiton Station

Thames Ditton Station

A307

0   1 km

© Crown copyright

and follow the path as it hugs the river bend. Beyond, to the left of the towpath, cows graze placidly in Petersham Meadows.

Peering through the trees on the far bank of the river, 200m beyond Petersham Meadows, is the splendid facade of **Marble Hill House**, a creamy Italianate confection built in 1729 for **Henrietta Howard**, the Countess of Suffolk, who was George II's mistress and lady-in-waiting to his wife, Queen Caroline. The *menage à trois* was no secret, and the two women were said to have "hated one another very civilly". Howard enjoyed a lavish lifestyle here, entertaining the likes of Alexander Pope and Horace Walpole in the extravagantly gilded reception rooms. These rooms are now ornately furnished with some fine period furniture.

Marble Hill House is open April–Sept daily 10am–6pm; Oct daily 10am–5pm; Nov–March Wed–Sun 10am–4pm; £3 (EH).

If you fancy visiting the house you can catch **Hammerton's Ferry** (daily 10am–6pm; 80p) across the river. The ferry runs from a well-marked spot on the riverbank a few hundred metres beyond Petersham Meadows, crossing on demand between Marble Hill and Ham House (see below). From the Richmond side of the river, the ferry runs to the foot of Orleans Road on the Twickenham side, from where it's a short walk downriver to Marble Hill. Marble Hill doesn't really compete with the attractions of Ham House and Hampton Court, however, and is probably best visited on a separate occasion.

Ham House

A hundred metres beyond Hammerton's Ferry, a tree-lined avenue runs up from the towpath to the main entrance of **Ham House** (late March to Oct Mon–Wed, Sat & Sun 1–5pm; gardens same days 10.30am–6pm or dusk; £5, garden only £1.50; NT). Built in 1610 for the first Earl of Dysart, the house was greatly expanded and lavishly decorated by Dysart's daughter, Elizabeth, and her second husband, the Earl of Lauderdale – the building works left the family heavily in debt, however, and little was changed over the following three hundred years by the cash-strapped Lauderdales, with the result that the house now survives as an unusually well-preserved period piece. In 1948, the National Trust acquired the house and began restoration, while the **gardens** have also recently been returned to their seventeenth-century glory. Features include a cherry garden, a "Wildernesse" (actually a maze-like area of hornbeam hedges concealing four circular summerhouses), a kitchen garden and an orangery, which now serves as a tearoom and makes a good place for **lunch**.

Eel Pie Island

0.5km

A couple of hundred metres beyond the grounds of Ham House you'll come to one of the largest islands on the Thames: **Eel Pie Island**. Pies and ale were sold on the island as far back as the sixteenth century – Henry VIII is said to have stopped off once en route between Whitehall and Hampton Court to sample the local fare – though the island didn't acquire its present name until the nineteenth century. The island's reputation as a spot for revelry and entertainment continued into the twentieth century, with steamers bringing day-trippers down the river from London – even the Rolling Stones played here during the 1960s. Today, the island is home to a bohemian community of artists and inventors, including Trevor Bayliss, the brains behind the wind-up radio.

The water around the island is surprisingly clear and you may even catch sight of the eels that gave the island its name.

The Ham Lands

2km

Beyond Eel Pie Island, the river meanders on, past gently sloping banks where small shingle beaches make ideal sites for a **picnic**. Inland, meadows stretch off to the horizon. There's a sense that the city hasn't yet encroached here, even though you're just a few hundred metres away from the northern reaches of Kingston-upon-Thames, while the suburbs of Twickenham and Teddington lie on the opposite bank, obscured by the trees.

Surprisingly, this apparently rural landscape is very much a product of its urban surroundings. Prior to World War II, the **Ham Lands** – the stretch of meadow flanking the Richmond side of the river between Ham House and Teddington Lock – was an ugly, industrial landscape, scarred with gravel pits. Land reclamation began here in the late 1940s, using rubble from bomb-damaged sites in central London, which was brought here to fill in the gravel pits. The made-up ground has been carefully managed ever since: looking at it today, it's hard to imagine that there was ever anything here but unspoiled countryside.

Teddington Lock to Kingston Bridge

3km

Roughly 2.5km beyond Ham House you come to **Teddington Lock**, a collective name for the series of locks and weirs that marks the end of the tidal river. Just beyond it, the suburb of **Kingston-upon-Thames** begins. The old towpath has been built over here, but the route continues close by the river, past a large green and on to probably the least pleasant stretch of the walk: the route under the railway and up onto Kingston Bridge. Keep close to the river and you'll find steps up onto the bridge just beyond a white, clap-boarded building, constructed on a platform over the river (it houses a *Slug & Lettuce* pub).

Hampton Court Park and Palace

4.5km

Head over Kingston Bridge and cross the road to reach the continuation of the towpath. You're now at the northeastern tip of **Hampton Court Park**, though there's little to see for a while apart from the suburban sprawl on the opposite bank. A few hundred metres on, the views open up to reveal the park, with the chimneys of the palace itself rising above the trees in the distance. This corner of the grounds is given over to a golf course, but the deer, which roam freely here as else-where in the park, appear unperturbed by the golf balls and plus-fours. Across the river, boathouses nestle by the opulent suburban homes of Surbiton.

With the final bend of the river on the approach to Hampton Court the vista opens up: the palace lies just ahead, with the village green at **Molesey** on the opposite bank. In summer this is a quintessentially English scene, with crick-eters playing on the green, people strolling or sitting by the river, and pleasure boats trawling the Thames.

Hampton Court Palace was built for Cardinal Wolsey in 1516 and purloined by Henry VIII thirteen years later. Cromwell moved in during the Commonwealth (he died here in 1658), and in 1838 Queen Victoria opened the palace to the public. Some of the most ambitious work was carried out in the late seventeenth century, during the reign of William and Mary, who hired Sir Christopher Wren to remodel the palace. Wren had planned to demolish the Tudor structure and rebuild in the style of Versailles, though his ambitious plans were brought to a halt by the death of Mary in 1684. The additions that he was able to make to the palace, including the king and queen's own apartments, form an interesting counterpoint to the original red-brick structure.

Entrance to the grounds is free, but to see the Royal Apartments you'll need a ticket – expensive, but well worth it. You can stroll around at your own pace, or take one of the excellent guided **tours** (price included in entry fee), although these only cover Henry VIII's State Rooms and the King's Apartments (William III's state apartments). It's also worth having a look at the **Tudor Kitchens** and **Wine Cellar**: the workaday underbelly of the palace, these offer a stark contrast to the opulent interiors upstairs. Henry VIII had the kitchens quadrupled to their current size, and they are kitted out as they would have been to cater for the massive banquets for which he was famous.

The palace's **grounds** cover almost seven hundred acres, but the main attraction, the famous **maze** (covered by ticket to the Royal Apartments; otherwise £2.10), lies close to the palace itself near the Lion Gates to the north of the complex. The maze is quite tricky – leave yourself plenty of time for getting lost if you plan on giving it a go.

Bushy Park

2km

From the palace, you can either catch a train back from **Hampton Court station** (just across the river by Hampton Court Bridge) or head back through **Bushy Park** – the entrance is opposite the Lion Gates at the northern boundary to the park – to Teddington station, 1.5km to the north. Bushy Park was Hampton Court's royal hunting park, and today is still home to abundant red and fallow deer, though with over a thousand acres to lose themselves in, you may see surprisingly few. The route to Teddington takes you along **Chestnut Avenue**, designed by Sir Christopher Wren and lined with 300-year-old horse chestnuts. On the far side of the park, head straight ahead down Avenue Gardens. At the T-junction at the end of Avenue Gardens bear right then first left down Victoria Road; **Teddington station** is in front of you.

London Loop

Old Bexley to Petts Wood

Distance and difficulty: 12km; easy to moderate.
Train: Charing Cross to Bexley (zone 6); return from Petts Wood
(zone 6) to Charing Cross or Victoria.
Map: OS Landranger 177: *East London*; OS Explorer 162:
Greenwich & Gravesend.

Created over the past decade, the **London Loop** is a 224–
kilometre walking trail that makes a complete circuit around
the edge of the capital, sticking for the most part to green
areas, to form a kind of walkers' M25. Starting in **Old
Bexley**, this part of the loop passes through the grounds of
Foots Cray Place and historic **Scadbury**, from whose
wooded hillside estate there are expansive views south across
the valley into the Kent countryside. Beyond Scadbury, the
walk passes through **Petts Wood**, a National Trust-protected
area of ancient woodland. **Lunch** options are sparse: either
take a picnic or try the *Brewer's Fayre* pub-restaurant in
Sidcup Place for a run-of-the-mill pub lunch.

Getting started

1.5km

Turn right out of **Bexley station** and walk down to **Bexley
High Street**. Turn right here and then almost immediately
right again, onto Tanyard Lane (just before the *Railway
Tavern*), following signs for the London Loop. Head down
Tanyard Lane and follow the track at the bottom of it under
the rail bridge and round to the right. The path flanks the
verge of the railway and runs past a cricket ground and an
isolated row of cottages before rising sharply up to some
fields.

The River Cray and Five Arches Bridge

1.5km

The fields cover the site of a former gravel pit (it's still being
refilled in one small corner over to the left) and is now a
popular recreation spot, with **Joyden's Wood** rising up on
the hillside to your left. After 750m the track over the fields
leads back down to housing at the eastern edge of **Sidcup**.
Just before the row of houses, bear left, following London
Loop waymarkers straight down to the tiny **River Cray**, a
shallow, crystal-clear stretch of water running over a pebble
bed into woodland.

Cross the river by the small footbridge and turn right, following the riverbank down past the edge of playing fields

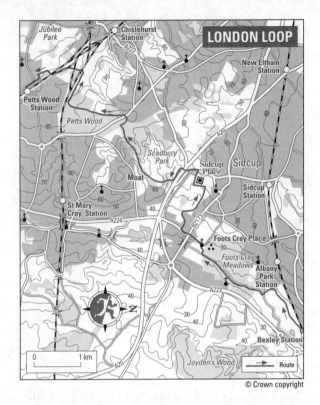

© Crown copyright

and into the trees. After a little over 750m you reach **Five Arches Bridge**, an elegant, stone span across a small weir which once formed part of the landscaped estate of **Foots Cray Place**, an eighteenth-century mansion that stood on the hill to the west until it burnt down in 1949. The estate is now a pleasant mix of meadow and parkland. Beyond the bridge, the river widens to form a small lake, which is home to swans and other water birds.

Foots Cray Meadows to Sidcup Place

3km

Carry on along the river for another 750m, through **Foots Cray Meadows**, until you reach a small footbridge. Cross the bridge over the river and go straight on for a few metres, then bear left following London Loop waymarkers just before a church to come out onto **Rectory Lane**. Turn left onto Rectory Lane and follow the road up to the crossroads and head straight across onto **Cray Road**. Take the second turning right after the crossroads along **Suffolk Road**, and then take the public footpath at the end of this cul-de-sac for a couple of hundred metres, skirting playing fields, and turn right onto a footpath leading past a paddock on your right.

At the end of the paddock, go through a kissing gate and bear left on the track beyond, heading past a scout hut and the end of a residential street (Oxford Road).

Continue along the track behind the houses to come out into **Sidcup Place Park**. This is part of the former estate of **Sidcup Place**, an eighteenth-century house which stands on the hilltop ahead, behind a clump of massive redwoods trees which were planted when the house was first built. Head straight uphill, across the clipped grass and passing a children's play area, to reach the house itself. Built in 1743, the original house was designed in the shape of a star fort, but was heavily modified and extended during the nineteenth century to resemble an Elizabethan manor house, with tall chimney breasts, a steep tiled roof and gabled fronts. It now houses a *Brewer's Fayre* **pub-restaurant**.

Scadbury Park

3km

Just before Sidcup Place, turn left along the path that runs along the edge of the garden terrace, turning right just beyond the terrace to head up the edge of an open grassy space to the A222 (Chislehurst Road) at the top of the rise. Turn left along the A222 and follow the pavement down towards **Frognal Corner** roundabout. Just before this busy road junction, where the A222 and A20 meet, there's a path down to an underpass; head down the path under the round-about, loop round to the left and over the A20 then down again and left under the approach road on the far side. Turn left here and continue along the path up towards the A20, following the pavement alongside it for a few metres before turning right and heading over a stile into Scadbury Park.

Head straight on, downhill to reach another track in the belt of trees ahead of you, then turn left and follow this track through the woods into heathland, joining another track and continuing on back into the trees, through a kissing gate and on, following London Loop waymarkers. At this point, you'll see the rolling landscape of **Scadbury Park** stretching away to your right. Overlooking the Cray Valley – an attractive tract of the Kent countryside – the wooded hill on which Scadbury (from the Old English *scead* and *burgh*) sits was for a long time thought to be the site of an Anglo Saxon fort; excavation has revealed nothing to verify this theory, however, and contemporary thinking is that the name simply means shady hill.

Follow the track up past a small pond in the trees to the left. A few hundred metres further on, bear sharp left just before a gate and follow the track signposted as the **Scadbury Park Circular Loop**. A hundred metres further on, turn right along a track which climbs up through the trees. At the top, another track leads off to the right. Follow this for a short detour to the site of **Scadbury Manor**. Dating from the late thirteenth century, the manor house was home first to the de Scathbury family, then passed to the Walsinghams a century later. The Walsinghams were a well-connected family: **Sir Francis Walsingham**, Elizabeth I's Secretary of State, was instrumental in bringing the conspiracy case against Mary Queen of Scots that led to her execution in 1586, while Sir Francis's nephew, **Thomas Walsingham**, invited **Christopher Marlowe** to stay at Scadbury to escape an outbreak of plague in London. It was here that the playwright was arrested on a charge of atheism. He was tried and found guilty at the nearby Palace of Nonsuch on May 20, 1593, but was bailed rather than imprisoned, thanks to some influential connections. Just ten days later, however, he died in suspicious circumstances in Deptford. The medieval manor was demolished in the eighteenth century, though you can still make out the moat and the boundaries of the old house.

Continue along this side track, passing the site of the manor house to your right, and you'll come back to the main track in less than a 100m. Turn right along the main track and head through birch wood for 750m to reach a grassy clearing, where several tracks meet. Carry straight on, ignoring the first path to your left, and head up towards a tarred lane. Ultimately, you need to turn left to head up this lane, but the 100m or so to the left of the woodland track is privately owned and closed to pedestrians. To detour round this section, take the minor track left through the woods 50m before the tarred lane. This leads in less than 100m to a T-junction; turn right here to head up to the lane on the far side of the private area. Turn left along it for a few metres to reach the busy A208.

Petts Wood

1.5km

Follow the track on the opposite side of the A208 for 300m until the track forks. Go right, following the London Loop waymarkers, and continue for 300m to reach a National Trust sign marking the edge of **Petts Wood**, a wonderfully wild and unkempt mix of oak, sweet chestnut and birch trees. The woods are probably named after the Pett family, master shipwrights from Deptford, who leased the area in the sixteenth century and farmed the woods for their prime oak.

Follow the main track downhill through the woods. After 100m you'll see a memorial off to your right to **Francis Joseph Fredrick Edlmann**, a founder member of the movement which saved the woods from developers in 1927. The track continues downhill towards a railway line; just before the tunnel under the railway, take the path that leads uphill to the right. A few metres on, take the left-hand fork and head downhill to a small footbridge, then head up again to take the another left-hand fork, heading through bucolic woodland surroundings which belie their proximity to the rail line.

Soon after the second left-hand fork the track drops down again and emerges at the edge of the trees; ahead lies meadowland. The track keeps close to the rail line here, skirting the edge of the meadows and following tiny **Kyd Brook** for a short way before crossing the brook and heading round and up over a footbridge across the railway.

To Petts Wood station

1.5km

On the far side of the footbridge, follow the pavement that leads straight on to a second footbridge over a second set of railway lines and then straight on to a suburban street (Little Thrift); cross this and continue straight on along the track opposite, between the houses. In 500m you come to a third footbridge, this one over an expansive tangle of rail track, on the far side of which is **Jubilee Country Park** – more suburban than country, but pleasant enough for all that. Turn left onto a track that leads through trees and past a car park to **Tent Peg Lane**, a short road that meets **Crest View Drive** at a T-junction. Turn left onto this well-to-do suburban street and follow it round a bend to the right, shortly after which it becomes **Queensway**, a parade of shops, off which, some 400m from Tent Peg Lane, is the turning for **Petts Wood station**.

The Parkland Walk

Finsbury Park to Alexandra Palace

Distance and difficulty: 8km; easy.
Train: Victoria Line tube or overground train from King's Cross to
Finsbury Park (zone 2); return by overground train from Alexandra
Palace (zone 3) to King's Cross.
Map: OS Landranger 176: *West London*; OS Explorer 173:
London North.

The **Parkland Walk** follows the course of the former **Great
Northern Railway**, which was dismantled and transformed
into a footpath in the mid-1980s. Starting in unprepossessing
Finsbury Park, the walk follows the leafy corridor of the former railway through cuttings and across embankments to
Highgate, then continues through **Queen's Wood** and
Highgate Wood, two remnants of the Forest of Middlesex,
the once-great tract of woodland that covered the whole of
the north London area. Beyond the woods, the walk resumes
along the course of a former branch line of the railway to the
sprawling Victorian **Alexandra Palace**. For **lunch**, the
Oshobasho Café in Highgate Wood is a good option.

Getting started

0.5km

Head out of the main exit at **Finsbury Park tube station** (follow signs for Station Place) and turn left across Stroud Green
Road. Opposite, just to the left of Rowan's tenpin bowling alley,
is the gated entrance to the Parkland Walk. Beyond the gate, a
path winds up to a track running between the present-day railway and the edge of Finsbury Park to reach a T-junction in a little under 500m; head left across the footbridge, then right to join
the course of the former Great Northern Railway. Note that the
first 500m of the walk is **currently closed**; for the present, you'll
have to turn left up Stroud Green Road, take the first right
(Woodstock Rd) and then the next right (Oxford Road), at the
end of which head up the steps onto the Parkland Walk.

Finsbury Park to Crouch End station

2.5km

Turn right, following the waymarkers, to join the course of
the disused railway, which climbs to higher ground behind
the houses. The path soon widens out, cutting a broad swathe
through the city sprawl, and starts to feel positively rural, with
the wooded hilltops of Highgate and Hampstead ahead of
you, and the suburban development on either side obscured
by trees and bushes.

Epping Forest

Queen Elizabeth's Lodge to Connaught Water

Distance and difficulty: 11km (shorter walk 5.5km); easy–
moderate.
Train: Liverpool Street to Chingford (every 20–30min; 30min);
return from Chingford to Liverpool Street (every 20–30min;
30min).
Map: OS Landranger 177: *East London*; OS Explorer 174: *Epping
Forest & Lee Valley*.

Starting in the northeast fringes of London, the ancient decid-
uous woodland of **Epping Forest** stretches along a high gravel ridge for almost twenty kilometres into the Essex countryside. Originally a royal hunting ground, Epping Forest was
opened to the public by the Epping Forest Act of 1878, since
when it has been managed by the Corporation of London.
Covering some six thousand acres, the forest is London's largest
public open space, and its sheer scale and raw beauty come as a
surprise to the first-time visitor, not least because of its proximity to the urban sprawl. It remains a popular spot, and at any
time of year you can expect to share the forest with plenty of
horseriders and cyclists, as well as many fellow walkers.

This circular walk heads from **Chingford station** up to
Queen Elizabeth's Hunting Lodge before heading north
into the heart of the forest. The midway point is the woodland village of **High Beach** – the *King's Oak* here makes a
good **lunch** stop. The second half of the walk takes you further east, past the Iron Age earthworks of **Loughton Camp**
and on to **Connaught Water**, the largest of the 150 ponds
that dot the forest. The route is along clear trails throughout,
though few of them are waymarked and the public footpaths
marked on the Ordnance Survey maps can be misleading
(we've indicated below any instances where there is likely to
be confusion). You can **shorten the walk** from 11km to
5.5km by deviating off the main route at the top of Long
Hills and rejoining it at Fairmead Road (see p.34).

Getting started

0.4km

From **Chingford station**, turn right onto Station Road (the
A1069). Almost immediately, **Chingford Plain** – the grassy
expanse on the forest's edge where royalty once hunted –
opens up before you, with the forest beyond. Follow the
main road as it heads uphill, keeping the plain on your left
and the large houses of Forest Avenue to your right.

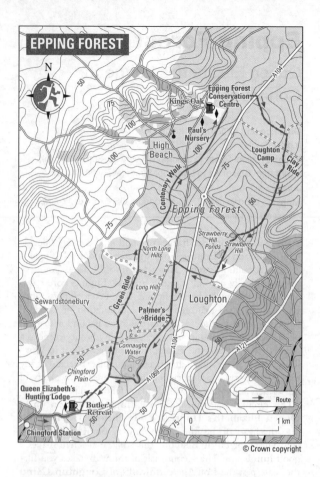

© Crown copyright

Queen Elizabeth's Lodge and Butler's Retreat

0.1km

At the brow of the hill, just beyond the mock-Tudor *Royal Forest* pub, **Queen Elizabeth's Hunting Lodge** comes into view. Built for Henry VIII in 1543, and renovated for Elizabeth I in 1589, the timber-framed lodge served as a grandstand from which hunts on the plain below could be watched – as such, it would originally have been open to the elements, though its timber frame was later enclosed with plaster. There's no evidence that either monarch ever actually used the building, but the association with Elizabeth stuck, and by the seventeenth century the lodge had acquired its present name. The lodge has been used variously as a law court, tearooms and a family home. It now houses a small **museum** (Feb–Oct Wed–Sun 2–5pm; Nov–Jan Sat & Sun 2pm until dusk; 50p), with low-key exhibits on the history of the building; as you'd expect, there are great views from the gallery across the plain, where hunts would have taken place.

Next door to the lodge lies **Butler's Retreat**, a traditional whitewashed and red-tiled Essex barn which was subsequently converted into a "forest retreat" (see box above) to cater for the crowds of urban pleasure-seekers who frequented the forest during the late nineteenth century.

....

Butler's Retreat (☏020/8524 2976) restaurant and snack bar serves inexpensive snacks and hot drinks (from the kiosk on the north side of the building) and more substantial meals, including filling breakfasts (served inside). There's also a fancier evening menu at weekends if you fancy an after-walk dinner.

....

Into the forest

3km

Turn left on the far side of *Butler's Retreat* and follow the path down between the retreat and the small **Butler's Retreat Pond** and on across Chingford Plain towards the forest. The path here, along with many of the tracks through the forest, is classified as a bridleway, so can become a bit churned up by the many horses that use it.

After some 500m you reach the edge of the forest and the ground becomes firmer underfoot. Follow the path as it runs dead ahead into the trees, forming an impressive avenue known as **Green Ride**. Head straight on for around 1.5km, passing straight over a crossroads after 500m and then making the gentle ascent up **Long Hills** to reach the summit of the ridge on which the bulk of the forest sits.

At the top of the hill, just beyond a left-hand turn, the main path bears off to the right; follow this for the **shorter loop** described below. To continue on the main route, take the second track, which carries straight on from this bend, over a small "crossroads" and up along the right-hand side of a small clearing, up **North Long Hills** and out of the trees to the edge of **Whitehouse Plain** – cows are often let out to graze here, reflecting the forest's status as common land. The path snakes its way north for 750m, up along the left-hand edge of the plain and then back into the trees to climb steeply uphill to a minor road.

If you want to cut the walk short here (reducing the
complete 11km to around 5.5km), continue along
Green Ride as it bears around to the right before
the clearing described in the main route. In a few
minutes you'll reach a north–south trail; turn left (north)
onto this to head round to Fairmead Road (see opposite).

Up and Down Ride to High Beach

1km

Cross the road and pick up the trail on its far side, which runs parallel to the busy A104, whose traffic can mar the forest's tranquility here, especially during the summer. The distant roar of traffic is more than compensated for, however, by the dramatic landscape here, as the trail – the aptly named **Up and Down Ride** – begins to rollercoaster through ancient coppiced and pollarded woodland.

A few metres beyond the final rise out of Up and Down Ride you pass the site of a former forest nursery, **Paul's Nursery**, over to your left. The nursery was reincorporated into the forest in 1920, though it's still home to exotic plant life found nowhere else in the forest, including foreign maples – spectacular in autumn – lilies of the valley, azaleas and rhododendrons.

Some 750m beyond Paul's Nursery, and a couple of hundred metres beyond a right-hand turn (to which we will return later), the track comes out on the road into High Beach village. Take the track to your left just before the road, on the near side of Oak Plain Pond, to reach the **Epping Forest Information Centre** (Easter–Oct Mon–Sat 10am–5pm; Nov–Easter Mon–Fri 11am–3pm, Sat & Sun 11am–5pm; ☏020/8508 0028). The centre has good displays on the forest's history, flora and fauna, and past and present management techniques. Behind the information centre lies the village of **High Beach**, little more than a clutch of houses, a green and a pub, the **King's Oak**, which offers filling bar meals; the attached kiosk serves takeaway tea, coffee and inexpensive hot and cold snacks.

Towards Loughton Camp

1.5km

From High Beach, retrace your steps back along the trail towards Up and Down Ride. Ignore all the wheelchair-access trails close to the information centre; after a few hundred metres, turn left at the first proper fork, just before Paul's Nursery. This muddy track takes you in around 400m to the busy **A104**, the main road through the forest.

Cross the road to the small car park opposite, then take the main track leading out of it, southeast into the forest. About 750m further on, this trail joins another heading south. Turn right onto this, passing the wide, grassy avenue of **Clay Ride** a few metres further on to your left (Centenary Walk, marked here on Ordnance Survey maps, is very overgrown, which can make map reading confusing).

A hundred metres or so south of Clay Ride, to the right of the trail, you should be able to make out the earthworks of the Iron Age settlement of **Loughton Camp**, a twelve-acre site that is now somewhat obscured by pollarded trees inside and around it. This is one of two earthworks in the forest (the other is Ambresbury Banks, in the northern reaches of the forest): it's thought that these sites were bolt holes for local people and their livestock during periods of tribal warfare, rather than permanently settled places.

Loughton Brook to Palmer's Bridge

2km

Past the camp's southern reaches the trail descends sharply down to tiny **Loughton Brook**, then rises steeply again towards the road into nearby Loughton. To the left of the trail you can see the brook twisting and turning as it meanders along the valley floor, carving out a surreal landscape of exposed tree roots and muddy flats.

Cross the Loughton Road and continue along the trail to the left of the man-made **Strawberry Hill Ponds**, created as fishponds in the nineteenth century and still used for fishing. Follow the track as it leads downhill, past fields and the greenhouses of Loughton nurseries to your left, to reach a trail to the right, 750m or so from the road and just after the second of the two ponds. Continue for another 750m to arrive back at the A104.

Cross the road, then take the trail to the right, which leads across heathland, skirting the northern side of the nearest trees before joining the old **Fairmead Road** (now closed to through traffic) a few hundred metres further on. Where you meet the road, a path leads off into the woods; this is where you'll come out if you took the short cut described earlier (see p.34).

Turn left onto Fairmead Road and head south for just under a kilometre to reach **Palmer's Bridge** to your right – a grand name for a couple of planks over a little ditch. Continue along Fairmead Road for another 10m or so and then take the path that bears right off it, by the edge of the trees.

On to Connaught Water

3km

Continue along the path, following the left bank of a tiny stream to **Connaught Water**, 750km beyond Palmer's Bridge, an attractive man-made lake which was created in 1893 by damming tiny Ching Brook and digging out the adjacent marshy area. The lake is very popular with day-trippers, even on the bleakest of winter days, and is also home to a rich variety of **wildfowl**, including the strikingly multi-coloured mandarin ducks which breed here over winter and which are easily spotted from early October through to spring.

Follow the circular path around the lake to the opposite side of the water, where a sluice marks the exit point of the tiny brook that feeds Connaught Water. Take the path down to follow the brook for a few metres before crossing it by way of a little wooden bridge. Head straight over the grassy clearing through the trees, across a gravelled path and back up hill to *Butler's Retreat*, which can be seen through the trees ahead. From here, retrace your steps back up to the main road, turn right and head downhill, past Queen Elizabeth's Hunting Lodge and Chingford Plain, to reach **Chingford station**.

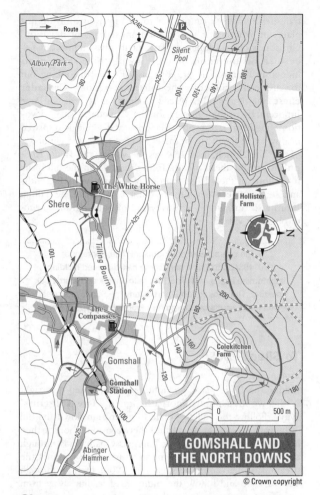

© Crown copyright

Shere

Follow the path along a line of the trees until you come to **Shere**. Follow the Millennium Trail sign to the right, through a gate which takes you to **St James' Church**, entered via a handsome lychgate by Lutyens. The church is mainly Norman, with a fine, plain interior and a beautiful font (dating from around 1200), its bowl patterned with scallop shapes. Inside the church on the north wall is a quatrefoil with a squint, which allowed the local anchoress, **Christine Carpenter**, to see the altar – her only view of the outside world. Christine was walled up in a cell attached to the church in 1329; she was released after three years, but later succeeded in having herself imprisoned again. Contemporary documents describe her desire to evade the "rapacious wolf" outside her cell – it's unclear whether she was guilty of some transgression which caused her to be imprisoned in the first place, or whether it was a self-imposed act of devotion. Christine's cell no longer exists, but its low outline can still be seen on the exterior wall, giving some sense of its hideously claustrophic proportions. Also worth looking out for inside the church is the thirteenth-century **Crusader chest**, one of a number placed in churches by order of Pope Innocent III to raise money for the Crusades; a small devotional medieval statue of a Madonna and Child is displayed nearby, while fragments of medieval glass adorn the windows.

From the church, head towards the village; the *White Horse* **pub** is straight ahead of you. To the right down the hill is the main body of the village, mostly comprising pretty fifteenth- and sixteenth-century timber-framed cottages. The Tilling Bourne stream, which is usually full of bobbing ducks, runs through the village.

The characterful and popular *White Horse* pub (☎01483/202518) is a handsome half-timbered building, labyrinthine inside, with fine Tudor stonework and sturdy oak seating. The cooked food, particularly the Sunday lunches, isn't great, so it's best to go for ploughman's-type options.

To Silent Pool

2km

Exiting the *White Horse*, go right, up the hill, then turn right at the wooden public footpath signed "**The Pilgrims' Way**". Follow the yellow public footpath sign down the hill – the path is paved at this point – between some houses, then head left at the yellow arrow. The grassy path leads through the trees; where the path emerges turn right towards the stream. Turn left along the stream for 100m, then go through Vicky's Gate and follow the minor road leading away from the stream, turning left onto the path after 500m.

After 200m you come out into a big field which opens up to reveal downland. Go through a stretch of beech and birch wood, and then cross a stile into a field. Off to the left, you can see the chimneys of **Albury Park**, a much altered Tudor manor house. After 200m you pass a very old church, then cross a stile, and descend the field towards the A248. At the road, turn right. A narrow path runs along the side of the road, saving you from having to walk on the road itself.

At the end of the road lies the busy, dual-carriageway **A25**. Turn left here, then cross the road almost immediately to reach first Sherbourne Pool and then **Silent Pool**. The two pools are pretty devoid of atmosphere, thanks to the roar from the A25, but a couple of signs attempt to drum up some interest, narrating the tale of a woodman's daughter who was bathing in the Silent Pool when a caddish noble-

After 250m you come to a stile on the left marked with a yellow arrow; ignore it and carry on straight ahead. After another 250m, the path curves left into woodland, and through an orchard. Cross a little bridge over a stream, and then follow the steep path up into **Harbledown**, mentioned in the *Canterbury Tales* as "Bob up and down", presumably for its hilly geography. The route joins a tarmac path; turn left and go straight ahead.

Into Canterbury

1.5km

The path comes out at a large roundabout; cross the road via the subway and go straight ahead, following the blue cycle-path sign to the city centre (you are now diverging from the official Pilgrims' Way to follow a more scenic route into the city). After 800m, go through the gate into **West Gate Gardens**, just right of the sign for Whitehall Road. Cross the footbridge over the Stour, turn left and walk through the gardens to emerge at the medieval **West Gate**. Many pilgrims ended their journey at a canter – the word derives from the phrase "at a Canterbury pace" – to reach the West Gate before dusk, when the portcullis descended. Turn right here and go straight up **Canterbury**'s main street, where there's an all-pervasive smell of fast food from the grotty selection of kebab and burger joints that has colonized the otherwise appealing mixture of old buildings. About 200m up the street, the road crosses the river – look up to the left and you'll see a **ducking stool**. Turn left at Boots, down narrow Mercery Lane, for the cathedral.

The Cathedral

Mercery Lane leads into the Buttermarket, where pilgrims once bought religious relics. Before you is the wonderfully elaborate sixteenth-century **Christ Church Gate**, and beyond that lies **Canterbury Cathedral** itself. Canterbury Cathedral has been central to the history of the English Church since St Augustine's sixth-century mission from Rome to establish Christianity in the country. The original Saxon church was rebuilt by **Archbishop Lanfranc** in the eleventh century, but was severely damaged by fire a hundred years later. The choir was then rebuilt by William of Sens, a French master-mason, and extended by his successor, William the Englishman, in the 1180s. The rebuilding and remodelling of the nave and aisles continued into the early fifteenth century.

....

Canterbury Cathedral is open Easter to Sept Mon–Fri 9am–6.30pm, Sun 12.30–2.30pm & 4.30–5.30pm; Oct to Easter Mon–Fri 9am–5pm, Sun 12.30–2.30pm & 4.30–5.30pm; £3.50. Evensong (during which admission is free) is at 5.30pm Mon–Fri & 3.15pm on Sun.

....

From a distance the cathedral appears rather ethereal, but close up what impresses is its colossal physical presence. The bulk and length of the Gothic nave is lightened by the soaring Bell Harry tower, added in the late fifteenth century. Inside, the stately **nave** is full of light, the ribs of its roof fanning out to join the long, central rib, punctuated by gold ceiling bosses. A flight of steps leads to the elaborate fifteenth-century choir screen, and beyond that another flight of steps ascends to the altar.

The **choir**, one of the longest in England, was built by the two Williams in transitional Norman style, with both round and pointed arches. It is separated from the aisles by ornate screens and canopied **tombs**. Amongst them are the splendid tomb of Henry IV (died 1413) and his second wife Joan of Navarre (died 1437), and a portrait effigy of Edward, the Black Prince (died 1376), hung with his flamboyant armour.

To the left as you face the choir screen is the area of the cathedral called "**Martyrdom**", where **Thomas Becket** was hacked to death as vespers were sung on December 29, 1170. A jagged modern sculpture symbolizes the bloody instruments of his murder. Becket, the Archbishop of Canterbury, had been chancellor and friend to **Henry II**, but they argued about the king's jurisdiction over the Church – few contemporary or modern commentators can explain Thomas's belligerence in reviving tensions between Church and state. Henry launched a furious outburst against Thomas, supposedly exclaiming, "Will no one rid me of this turbulent priest?" This, perhaps the most famous rhetorical question in English, prompted four knights to cross the Channel to kill the archbishop.

Stricken with guilt, Henry II did penance for the murder in the cathedral and soon after the English defeated the Scots at the battle of Alnwick, the first of a series of "miracles" which were associated with the shrine. Thomas was **canonized** three years after his death, and his lavish tomb became the most significant pilgrimage site in England. The tomb was destroyed by Henry VIII during the dissolution of the monasteries, but the cult of Thomas survived. To the east of the cathedral lies the spacious fourteenth-century chapter-house, where T. S. Eliot's austere verse play *Murder in the Cathedral* was first performed in 1935.

The lofty arched **crypt** features lively Norman carving on its capitals – the stonemasons, perhaps as a form of spiritual insurance, incorporated some distinctly pagan figures into the mix. The **Great Cloister** features beautiful Early English arcading; beyond it is a series of rambling buildings belonging to the King's School, a monastic foundation established in the seventh century – the Elizabethan playwright Christopher Marlowe was a pupil.

Leaving Canterbury

1km

There are two train stations in Canterbury – **Canterbury West**, just outside the West Gate, from where trains leave for London Bridge, and **Canterbury East**, where faster trains leave for Victoria (change at Ashford for a quicker journey). To reach Canterbury East, go up the High Street till you reach the roundabout and the city walls. Turn right and walk round the walls, the handsome **Dane John Gardens** down to the right. After 700m, a footbridge leads to the left, over the busy road that circles the walls, taking you right in to the station.

3

The South Downs

The "blunt, bow-headed, whale-backed" **South Downs**, as Kipling described them, run from Winchester in the west, terminating in the east at the spectacular high white cliffs near Eastbourne. Walking along the ridge of the downs, with the crescents of smooth, green-gold hills ahead, the sea to one side and the winding rivers to the other – and maybe a trilling skylark above – you can feel an exhilarating sense of space and isolation. The vegetation is low and from a distance appears sparse, lending the landscape rather an austere quality – the beauty, as far as plant-life goes, is in the detail, from butter-coloured cowslips to tiny, delicate orchids. The downs are cut through by a series of river valleys – the Arun, the Ouse, the Adur and the Cuckmere – dotted with wonderful medieval villages which, partly owing to the economic depression that characterized the area until intensive farming was begun after World War II, remain remarkably unchanged and unspoilt, and which offer plenty of diversions, from Saxon churches to excellent old country pubs.

All the walks in this chapter are in Sussex, around the less-developed eastern part of the downs. The first walk leads between the steep walls of the downs, following the lush banks of the **Arun** river towards Arundel's extraordinary castle and cathedral. The **Mount Caburn** walk ascends the downs from Lewes, dipping into the villages of Gynde and Firle, and including a detour to Charleston, the home of Vanessa Bell and Duncan Grant. The final walk in this chapter is a loin-girding two-day stomp (though you can easily treat it as two separate one-day walks) along the **South Downs Way**, from Falmer to Rodmell on day one, and then on to dramatic Beachy Head, via Alfriston and the Cuckmere Valley, on day two.

Trains for all these walks leave from Victoria, stopping at Clapham Junction, and take around an hour. The Mount Caburn walk is probably the best option if you want to **drive** – you can park at Lewes and then take the train for the very short journey back there from Southease. For all these walks aim **to start** by around 11am to get to the recommended pub for lunch, with the exception of the extremely long second day of the South Downs Way, which you'll need to start at around 9.30am.

Along the Arun

South Stoke via Burpham to Arundel

Distance and difficulty: 11.5km; moderate.
Trains: London Victoria to Amberley (hourly; 1hr 10min); return from Arundel to London Victoria (hourly; 1hr 25min).
Map: OS Landranger 197: *Chichester & the South Downs*; OS Explorer 121: *Arundel & Pulborough*.

Winding through the lush Arun Valley, this route links three ancient Sussex settlements: picturesque **South Stoke**, tucked in a bend of the Arun, with its lovely Saxon church; **Burpham**, which sits above the river and was fortified during the Danish invasions of the area during the tenth century; and **Arundel** itself, whose fantastic Gothic castle dominates the valley. It's best to time your walk to have **lunch** at the *George & Dragon* in Burpham. Bear in mind that the path can become very waterlogged.

Amberley to Arundel Park

2.5km

Emerging from **Amberley station**, turn left down the road, past the telephone box and take another left towards the long stone bridge; to the right are some little shops and cafés – the *Broughton Bridge Tea Gardens* has outside seating by the river and is a good place to fuel up before you start the walk.

Cross the bridge over the Arun. You'll see two green public footpath signs to the left – take the second one, at the end of the bridge, and then cross the stile into a **meadow** which borders the river (it can get very splashy underfoot). A path to the right leads up to a small flint church, but keep going straight ahead across the meadow, to an overgrown area on the far side, where a bridge leads over a brook. From here the path runs along the gently flowing **Arun**, bordered on either side by nettles, elderflower trees and – in June – banks of dog roses, irises and buttercups mixed in with the wild foliage. Dense reeds run down the river side of the path. Just over 750m from the start of the path, a large beech tree stands on the slope to the right, with intricate exposed roots and a rope swing.

To South Stoke

1.5km

Just past the swing the path opens out, with chalky cliffs to the right and the houses of North Stoke visible on the other

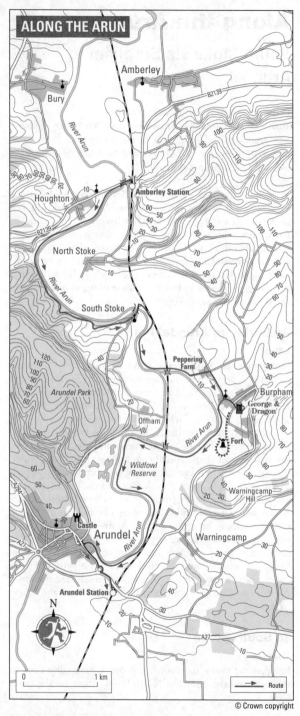

ALONG THE ARUN

side of the river. At the point where the river widens you'll reach the flint boundary wall of **Arundel Park**, created in 1806 by Charles, Duke of Norfolk, out of common land. Farmers lost the right to graze their sheep here, with the result that prosperity – and eventually the local population – declined sharply. Don't go through the gate into the park, but carry on along the path, keeping the flint wall to your right. The path begins to climb away from the river, zigzagging upwards to a stile where you cross over into a field.

The view now opens out, with a sloping field to the right, and the South Downs beyond. Carry on down the field and follow the farm track to the left, through a gate where you'll see a wooden public bridleway sign.

The path climbs up through woodland, then continues through a field to reach a farmyard. You're now in the village of **South Stoke**, which was owned by the earls of Arundel from the Norman Conquest till the reign of Elizabeth I. When Earl Philip Howard (later St Philip) refused to renounce Catholicism, his possessions – including South Stoke – were seized by the Crown. After years of imprisonment, he eventually died in the Tower of London.

Go past the mid-Victorian Chapel Barn, just beyond the farmyard, and turn left on the tarred road and left again to the beautiful flint church of **St Leonard's**. Although restored in the nineteenth century, St Leonard's is essentially Norman, with an aisle-less nave. The interior is appealingly rudimentary – the church has no electricity – and features a wonderful wooden-beamed ceiling. The churchyard is exceptionally pretty; the Georgian facade of the **rectory** conceals a house dating back to the fourteenth century.

To Burpham

2.5km

Turn right at the end of the narrow path leading to the church, then right again at the wooden public footpath sign (the fallen trees by the river here provide good seating for a **picnic**). Cross the metal bridge over the Arun then take a right over the wooden stile immediately beyond. You're now walking along a raised bank of the river, which is wide and fast-moving. Cross a wooden stile and pass through dense foliage; if it's too overgrown, just climb down the bank and carry on through the metal gate – either way you'll emerge into a stretch of **pasture**.

Continue along the bank of the river. Where the river splits, head up to another wooden stile where the route crosses the railway line towards Burpham. On the other side there's a pretty meadow; the river is much narrower and slower-moving at this point. When you meet the track, take the left-hand fork up the **hill**, passing a tumbledown brick and flint house on the right-hand side. Carry on up the track, which merges with a tarred road; follow the road and, where it divides, turn right opposite the sign for Peppering Farm.

From here you'll see the fairy-tale shape of **Arundel Castle** to the right across the valley with, bizarrely, a field of bison in the foreground. (Bison meat is low in fat and cholesterol and high in protein, and is marketed as a healthy alternative to the beleaguered domestic bovine.)

Burpham

Carry on along the road to enter **Burpham** (pronounced "Burfam"); turn left at the bottom of the road for the **pub**. Like South Stoke, Burpham is an extremely old settlement and the site of one of the five **forts** built by King Alfred (see box on p.124) to repel Danish invaders who used to sail up the Arun Valley, which was then a tidal estuary.

Burpham Church was substantially rebuilt between 1160 and 1220, the vaulted chancel being emphatically French in style, though the north wall of the nave and parts of the walls between the arches predate the Norman Conquest. A fine old copper beech stands in the churchyard, where you'll find the grave of the writer **Mervyn Peake**, who lived in the village; Gormenghast Castle in Peake's outlandish Gothic fantasy *Titus Groan* was inspired by Arundel Castle.

Just up the road from the church, the *George & Dragon* (☎01903/883131) makes a perfect lunch stop, serving fine bar snacks as well as upmarket – and expensive – three-course Sunday lunches. Wash it all down with a pint of Burpham Best Bitter.

Across the Arun Valley

5km

From the *George & Dragon*, head back past the church, but instead of turning right and retracing your steps, go straight ahead down the road with the dead-end sign. Turn left where the wooden public footpath sign points in two directions, and follow the path through the woods; the river now lies to your right and the raised ground up to the left conceals the remains of Alfred's **fort**. Excavations here have revealed the foundations of Saxon buildings, as well as the remains of a mint, which operated up until the Norman Conquest, but there's little to see now – just a wooded mound.

Beyond here, the path emerges at a stile. Cross this, ignoring the track that climbs up the hill to the left, and follow the path as it heads down a meadow and across the **Arun Valley**, with Arundel Castle straight ahead. Over to the left you'll see the terraces of **Warningcamp Hill**, possibly built and named by ancient Britons who feared Roman invasion.

The path continues, passing over dykes via a series of stiles and bridges, and crossing the railway line once more. Ahead, across the river, is the *Black Rabbit* pub at Offham, idyllically situated with a white cliff rising up behind and boats moored in front; Turner painted a mist-shrouded Arundel Castle from this point. Beyond here the path continues to run alongside the river – which is very wide at this point – as it curves away from Arundel, back towards Warningcamp. The surrounding area belongs to the Wildfowl and Wetlands Trust and harbours several unusual species, including the blue duck and the world's rarest goose, the nene, a black-and-grey short-winged Hawaiian bird.

You approach the railway line again but, instead of crossing it, climb over the stile marked by a post with yellow arrows, and continue round to the right. Cross over the V-shaped wooden stile; you're now heading back towards the castle. Up ahead, the busy **A27** breaks the peace – the path skirts it, curving round towards the town. Approaching Arundel, the river lies to your right, with little boats in various states of decay moored to fragile wooden jetties.

Arundel

The castle and nineteenth-century cathedral lose much of their Gothic glamour on closer inspection, being clearly faux-medieval, but nevertheless **Arundel** is a pretty little town, sitting on a hill in the middle of the Arun valley. Once an inland port linked to the sea by the Arun, Arundel's current staid atmosphere belies the fact that it was a vibrant shipbuilding centre until the Edwardian period, and was also the scene of fights between smugglers and excisemen.

If you want to skip the town and head straight for the **train station**, cut through the car park to the left of the riverside path, just before it emerges into Arundel. Head down to the busy road, and cross over, with the police station straight ahead; then take a left, continue down the road to the roundabout, and follow the A27 to the left. The station lies 200m up the A27 on the right-hand side.

Arundel Castle

Arundel Castle (April–Oct Mon–Fri & Sun noon–5pm; £9) was originally a Norman structure, but was blown up during the Civil War and lavishly reconstructed in the 1860s by Henry, fifteenth Duke of Norfolk, an immensely wealthy eccentric who dined on swans but dressed like a tramp. Inside the castle, make a beeline for the lofty **Baron's Hall** and the **library**, which is hung with works by Gainsborough, Holbein and Van Dyck. The fourteenth-century **Fitzalan Chapel** contains the tombs of past dukes of Norfolk, including two effigies of the seventh duke – one depicting him as he was when he died, the other his emaciated corpse. The chapel adjoins the fourteenth-century parish church of

St Nicholas, entered from London Road; the chapel is, very unusually, separated from the altar of the Anglican church by a glass screen and an older iron grille.

Arundel Cathedral

West from here along London Road is **Arundel Cathedral**, gloriously French-looking and romantic from a distance, but rather dull close up. Built in the 1870s by Duke Henry, the cathedral's spire was designed by John Hansom, inventor of the hansom cab. Inside is the tomb of St Philip Howard (see p.71), exhumed from the Fitzalan Chapel after his canonization in 1970.

Mount Caburn and the South Downs

Lewes to Southease, via Firle

Distance and difficulty: 14.5km; strenuous.
Trains: London Victoria to Lewes (every 30min; 1hr); Southease to Lewes (hourly; 8min); return from Lewes to London Victoria (hourly; 1hr 5min).
Maps: OS Landranger 198 and 199: *Brighton & Lewes* and *Eastbourne & Hastings* (the latter map is only needed if you do the detour to Charleston Farmhouse); OS Explorer 122 and 123: *Steyning to Newhaven* and *Newhaven to Eastbourne*.

This walk takes in the most pleasing features of the Sussex countryside: unspoilt villages, undulating chalky downland and a fine pub. From the busy town of **Lewes**, it climbs **Mount Caburn**, with its Iron Age earthworks, then descends to the idyllic villages of **Glynde** and **Firle**, both complete with cricket greens and delightful seventeenth- and eighteenth-century buildings. The *Ram* at Firle can provide a hearty **lunch**. From Firle there's a great detour through the grounds of Firle Place and across the fields to **Charleston Farmhouse**, the country retreat of the Bloomsbury Group. Beyond Firle, a steep path leads up onto the downs, with the **South Downs Way** running east for 5km along a high ridge to the village of Southease, from where there are trains to Lewes. Alternatively, to **shorten the walk**, return to Glynde from Firle and take the train back to Lewes from there.

Getting started

1.5km

Exit **Lewes station** and follow the way-out sign into town. Turn right almost immediately at the pub onto Landsdowne Place, then go straight ahead at the roundabout and turn right at Boots onto the High Street. Carry on to the junction and then go straight ahead up steep and narrow Chapel Hill. At the top of the hill, with the golf club on your left, is a wooden waymarker with yellow arrows. Follow this, crossing the stile, and turn left, following the fence for a short distance, then go straight ahead across the field, between two wooden posts and down into the valley.

Over Mount Caburn

3km

This is where the walk proper begins, through the valley that bisects **Mount Caburn**. There are no views from here,

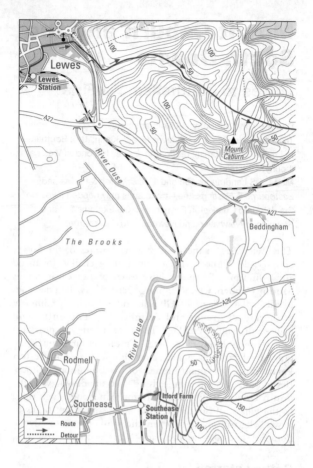

but the enclosing valley walls create a wonderfully still atmosphere, which intensifies the sound of lark song. Look out for yellow cowslips in April and May. Head downhill, crossing two stiles, then continue down across a field. Go straight ahead at a third stile by some feeding troughs, then follow the bottom of the slightly ridged hill round to your right. Cross yet another stile, after which the path begins to climb steeply.

At the top of the hill you cross one last stile, from where there's a panorama of the long ridge of the South Downs, the route of the second half of the walk. A short detour to the right leads to the fort itself, whose encircling **defensive ditches** are still clearly visible. Caburn (from the Celtic *caer bryn*, or "fortified hill") was the site of an Iron Age fort, erected around 500 AD. The fort is thought to have contained about seventy wattle-and-daub houses, gathered around a great hall.

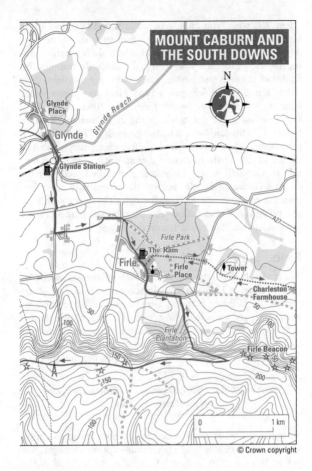

Glynde

3km

Return to the stile on the top of the ridge, then go right and down the hill to the village of **Glynde**, following the path which leads straight ahead. Glynde lies just to the south of the world-famous **Glyndebourne Opera House**, and is also home to Glynde Place, a fine Elizabethan mansion.

Entering the village you emerge from the path onto a paved road, with an attractive pink cottage opposite. Turn left then right onto Glynde's main street where, amongst the beautiful flint cottages, there's an Arts-and-Crafts-era working forge, fronted by a giant horseshoe (visitors are welcome). Pass Glynde **train station** on the right, cross the bridge over Glynde Reach, a tributary of the Ouse, and carry on past the *Trevor Arms*. Cross the busy A27 and take the narrow paved track directly ahead of you.

Turn left when you come to a wall marked Preston Court. Continue along the track, passing a flint barn and some out-buildings on your left, just beyond which there's a stile (also on the left). Cross the stile, turn right and walk through the field. Go through two sets of gates and cross the field, then swing round to the left, past a barn. Here you join a wider farm track; turn right towards Firle. After 300m, at the five-way junction, take the track to the right, marked "public footpath". This leads you into the grounds of **Firle Place**, a picturesque house built in the late fifteenth century, tucked in the lee of the downs to protect it from strong winds and fur-nish it with well water; it was later remodelled and given an elegant Georgian facade. Follow the paved path for 50m, then cut off down the path on the right. Go over the stile by the playground and follow the path between the cricket ground and the tennis courts into the village.

Firle

The route brings you out at the back of the seventeenth-century *Ram* at **Firle**, an ideal **lunch** or tea stop. The oldest part of the building is thought to be medieval, and there is, needless to say, a resident ghost, that of an old washerwoman with a wooden leg who lived in an attic in the eaves. She was found dead one day in her laundry basket, and it's claimed she can sometimes be heard stomping across her tiny room.

....

The *Ram* (☎01273/858222) serves excellent lunches, local ales and afternoon teas.

....

To rejoin the walk, carry on up Firle's main street, past rows of neat seventeenth- and eighteenth-century cottages. Just before you come to St Peter's Church at the top end of the village, there's a detour (2.5km each way) left off the main street to **Charleston Farmhouse**, the painter Vanessa Bell's immaculately restored home, which was a focus for the activ-ities of the Bloomsbury Group.

Detour to Charleston Farmhouse

5km

Go through the gate into the grounds of Firle Place and head to the right, passing the house which lies to your right. There are a couple of wooden posts with yellow arrows in the field showing the route through the estate, though they're easy to miss; you need to head for the high ground to the right, which is surmounted by a tower. At the edge of the estate go through the wooden gate up the driveway between two flint cottages, and then through a metal gate. Carry on ahead along the thin chalk path that leads up the field, to the right of the flint wall. At the top go through the wooden gate (a

chalk track heads left to the tower, which is a private house).
From the wooden gate, carry on straight ahead on the chalk
track that leads across the fields. From here you can see the
barns and orange roof of Charleston ahead of you.

Charleston Farmhouse

In 1916, on the recommendation of her sister Virginia Woolf,
Vanessa Bell moved to **Charleston Farmhouse**, along with
Duncan Grant, her two children and the writer David
Garnett. The house initially provided a rural retreat from
World War I, but soon became the country home of the
Bloomsbury Group and a social and artistic stimulus for
the Woolfs and other intellectuals including the artist and
curator Roger Fry, the biographer Lytton Strachey and the
economist John Maynard Keynes.

Charleston Farmhouse is open May, June, Sept & Oct
Wed–Sun 2–6pm; July & Aug Wed–Sat 11.30am–6pm,
Sun 2–6pm; £6; Ⓦwww.charleston.org.uk.
One-hour tours run every 20min.

Grant and Bell decorated every surface of Charleston –
both were admirers of the emphatic lines and bold colours of
the Post-Impressionists – so that the house became a work of
art in its own right. However, by the time Duncan Grant
died in 1978, Charleston had become dilapidated, and a rev-
erential **restoration** of the house and garden was undertak-
en. The Mediterranean colours of the wall paintings were
revived, perhaps the loveliest being the cock and hound
above and below Bell's bedroom window, which Grant painted to wake her in the morning and guard her at night. Some
of the experiments in the decorative arts were less successful,
as the rather wobbly pottery of the off-shoot **Omega
Workshop** testifies. But the house is still permeated with
sensuous colour and light, and the lush gardens, with their
quirky statuary, are enticing too; all can be seen on the
impressively informative tours.

On to the downs

1.5km

From Firle, continue up the main street, passing the drive to
St Peter's Church and the tradesmen's entrance to Firle Place,
and following the bridlepath signs. (If you've made the
detour to Charleston Farmhouse, you could simply turn left
up the track on the eastern edge of Firle Park and climb up
onto the downs from there). Follow the road, which curves
round to the left, for 500m, and then go along the faint path
up the hill to the right, skirting the aspen and silver birch
woods of **Firle Plantation** on your right. The path makes

the dizzying ascent up the escarpment of the South Downs, eventually joining the **South Downs Way** at the top. When you reach the top, the English Channel is revealed to the south; you might see a cross-channel ferry from Dieppe nipping into the port of Newhaven.

The South Downs Way

5.5km

At the top, take a right onto the **South Downs Way**, and continue for 300m till you come to a car park. From here the South Downs Way leads through a wooden gate marked with a sky-blue arrow and runs along the top of the ridge. There's no chance of losing your way here: just keep to the highest ground. After 700m you pass some radio masts on the left; from here the fort surmounting Mount Caburn is clearly visible.

After 1.5km, you start to descend, with Newhaven visible to the left. The track then plunges steeply, down Itford Hill towards **Southease**, to emerge onto the A26. Turn right here, then after 50m take the left-hand turn at Itford Farm, and carry on to **Southease station**, from where trains make the short run back to Lewes. Alternatively, you can call a **taxi** on ⓣ01273/477015 to take you back to Lewes (around £7).

The South Downs Way

Falmer to Eastbourne via Alfriston

Distance and difficulty: day 1: 14.5km; day 2: 34.5km; strenuous to very strenuous.
Trains: London Victoria to Falmer (via Lewes; every 15min; 1hr 38min); Eastbourne to London Victoria (every 30min; 1hr 30min).
Map: OS Landranger 198 and 199: *Brighton & Lewes* and *Eastbourne & Hastings*; OS Explorer 122 and 123: *Steyring to Newhaven* and *Newhaven to Eastbourne*.

The **South Downs Way** runs for 160km, from Winchester to Eastbourne; the two-day section described here covers the spectacular eastern extent of the route. It starts from **Falmer**, on the outskirts of Brighton, and ends at **Eastbourne**: each day's walk can be done separately, or you can stay at the youth hostel in Telscombe and make a two-day walk of it. On **day one**, the downland scenery is for the most part gentle rather than dramatic. **Day two** leads – via a couple of venerable Sussex villages – to the undulating cliffs at Beachy Head. The second day is extremely strenuous, and should only be undertaken if you're fit: there are a lot of kilometres and some fantastically wiggly contours to contend with.

When buying a **train ticket**, it's best to get a return to Lewes if you're just doing the first day, and then a single on to Falmer and a single from Southease back to Lewes. If you're doing both days, get a return to Eastbourne and buy a single on from Lewes to Falmer to start the walk. The alternative is to go to Falmer on the Brighton line, returning to London on the separate Lewes–Eastbourne line, but you have to buy two single tickets rather than a return, which is more expensive.

Day one

14.5km, plus 3km detour to Rodmell

Starting in **Falmer**, day one leads over the downs to the village of **Kingston**, where the *Juggs Inn* makes a decent **lunch** stop – this is a rewarding but longish detour, so to save a bit of effort you could bring a picnic. A breathtakingly steep climb leads you back onto the main ridge of the downs, which you follow to **Mill Hill**, from where there are sweeping views ahead to the sea. If you want to finish the walk at this point, you can descend from the ridge into **Rodmell**, where Virginia Woolf's weatherboarded home, **Monk's House**, can be visited, and from where buses run into Lewes; the alternative is to walk a little further on to **Southease** and catch the train to Lewes from there. If you want to stay on

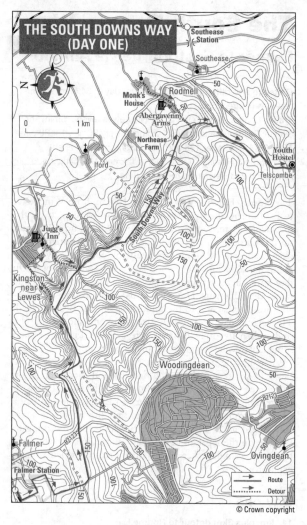

THE SOUTH DOWNS WAY
(DAY ONE)

Southease Station

Southease

Monk's House

Rodmell

Abergavenny Arms

Northease Farm

Iford

Youth Hostel

Telscombe

Jugg's Inn

South Downs Way

Kingston near Lewes

Woodingdean

B2123

Falmer

B2123

Ovingdean

Falmer Station

0   1 km

Route
Detour

© Crown copyright

the South Downs Way for a second day, tiny **Telscombe** is home to a basic but picturesque youth hostel.

Getting started

1km

Exit **Falmer station** from the platform that the Lewes train arrives on, rather than crossing the footbridge to the main part of the station. Walk down the platform away from the footbridge, take the path which exits the platform and turn right to follow it for 250m. The path then curves to the left towards a sports centre. Keep this immediately to your right, and head up to the road to a T-junction (there's a car park on your right). Go straight ahead at the T-junction, crossing the large rectangular playing field ahead of you, then go over the stile at the far left-hand corner of the field and follow the path up to the right, through a patch of woodland.

On to the Downs

6km

You emerge, after just 100m, into a field. Turn right and walk alongside the trees to the end of the wood, where there's a wooden post with a faded yellow sign – turn left here to climb up the hill. The path dips, and there's another steep climb – 500m beyond the woodland there's a wooden post with a blue arrow; ignore this and continue for a further hundred metres, then take a left instead of carrying on down the hill, keeping the fence to your right. From here the views begin to open out, and the downland, where it isn't cultivated, is scattered with wild flowers in spring and summer.

After 800m you cross a road, after which the route continues along the grassy track, following the public bridleway sign; 750m further on there's a path leading up to the right, marked with a blue arrow; ignore this and press on for another 100m to a patch of gnarled woodland, with a path leading down through it. Instead of following this path, turn up to the right for 50m on a path which then leads onto the officially designated (and signposted) **South Downs Way**.

Go through the double gates on to the South Downs Way and climb up the hillside for 500m, and then turn left at the top through the wooden gate. The track runs for just over a kilometre from here, the **downland** falling away dramatically to the left, to give terrific views over to Lewes. You go through a wooden gate – the South Downs Way continues up to the right. If you don't want to detour to Kingston, simply carry on along the route from here, and see p.84 – the middle of the "To Mill Hill" section – to continue.

Detour to Kingston

2km

Go straight ahead at the gate if you want to detour to **Kingston** for the pub. As you approach Kingston, the folds of the downs become more exaggerated; they are cloaked with emerald green grass where they are too steep for cultivation, giving some sense of what this landscape would have looked like when it was primarily used for grazing sheep, before the heavy cultivation that commenced following World War II.

A chalk and flint track leads down the hill to the edge of the village, which sits in a hollow. At the signpost with three bridleway signs, take the leafy path down the slope to the right on the edge of the village – this leads for 500m, skirting the modern part of the village, a large green and some tennis courts. Follow the path round to the left, towards the church.

Kingston

Kingston is very much a village of two halves, with featureless 1960s development surrounding a medieval core. The ancient part of the village comprises a fourteenth-century **church** (with a vividly coloured modern window, dedicated by Archbishop Tutu, commemorating the anti-apartheid campaigner Rev Michael Scott); a couple of handsome Georgian manor houses; and around twenty gentrified Tudor farmworkers' cottages. Head straight down the main street of the old village to reach the *Jugg's*, 100m beyond the church.

The *Jugg's* (℡01273/472523) is housed in two fifteenth-century cottages, the low-ceilinged interior complete with original beams and panelling. There's a garden out front for summer days, and it's snug inside in the winter.

To Mill Hill

5km

From the pub, turn right and go straight up the main street. Follow this, then turn left after 400m into the wood, over the stile. It's an extremely steep scramble from here up the grassy escarpment of the downs, over a couple of stiles. After 400m the path joins another track; turn right for a few metres, then left, to rejoin the **South Downs Way** itself. From here, the wide chalky track cuts a broad swathe through the fields, with views of Beachy Head in front of you. The track is crossed by a few farm roads, but just continue straight along the ridge of the downs – just be sure, when you join the concrete path, to follow the arrow to the left rather than going straight ahead. Some 2.5km beyond this point, you join a narrow fenced path which emerges at **Mill Hill** – Mill Hill house is at the end of the path on the right.

Detour to Rodmell

3km

If you want to end the walk after the first day, or if you want to detour to the village to see Monk's House and visit the pub, you need to turn left at Mill Hill instead of continuing on the South Downs Way, and follow the farm track for 750m, downhill to the village. The track emerges opposite the *Abergavenny Arms*; to reach the main part of the village, cross the road and go straight ahead. The small twelfth-century **church** and **Monk's House** (April–Oct Wed & Sat 2–5.30pm; £2.60; NT), the weatherboarded house where Leonard and Virginia Woolf lived and worked, are at the far end of this road. Inside, Virginia's writing table overlooks the

Ouse, where she drowned herself. There's a small exhibition of photographs, and excerpts from Virginia's letters and diaries.

The *Abergavenny Arms* **pub** is decent, and serves an excellent local organic beer – "Natural Blond". You can buy booze here if you're heading off for an evening at the youth hostel in publess Telscombe.

To **return to Lewes** from here, either catch the bus (they leave across the road from the *Abergavenny Arms*) or, facing the pub, turn right and continue down the road for 1.5km to **Southease** station, from where you can catch a train to Lewes (hourly; 8min); follow the signpost to Southease, left off the main road, and walk through the village and beyond, crossing the River Ouse. You can call a **taxi** to take you from Rodmell to Lewes (around £6) on ☎01273/477015.

To Telscombe

2.5km

To reach **Telscombe**, go straight ahead at Mill Hill instead of turning left; the path leads off the downs and into a valley, where you'll see a large **farm**. At the junction, the South Downs Way itself leads off to the left; to reach Telscombe turn right, walking through the farm. Follow the track which climbs up through farmland and then joins a road – turn right to get to the tiny, gentrified village, which consists of a handful of attractive old houses and a church with a mid-twelfth-century nave and chancel.

The village was said to have been occupied entirely by smugglers during the eighteenth century. In 1794, the *Sussex Weekly Advertiser* described the seizure of 51 barrels of liquor in a purpose-built cavern in the village. The officers and the women of the parish cracked open one of the barrels and "sipped so largely of the enlivening extract that they found themselves stimulated . . . and if one may judge from appearances, the liquor had suffered no diminution in its double distillation." The correspondent adds, circumspectly, that the "good dames of Telscombe conducted the process with as much modesty and decorum as the situation would admit of".

In the early twentieth century, the village came under the more respectable patronage of abstemious **Ambrose Goram**. He left the entire village to the Brighton Corporation in 1933, but attached a number of stringent conditions to the bequest: it's thanks to his legacy that there's no pub in Telscombe.

Telscombe Youth Hostel ☎01273/301357, ⓦwww.yha.org.uk; £10.25 per person) is housed in a row of eighteenth-century flint cottages on the left as you enter the village – beautiful from the outside, though nothing of the original interior remains. There's a small shop and reasonable cooking facilities.

Day two

34.5km

You'll need to get an early start to manage day two before dark. To do this as a one-day walk from London, you'd have to get an early train to Southease (hourly; 1hr 30min). It's a hugely rewarding walk, taking in some spectacular downland; a choice of two ancient inns at Alfriston for **lunch**; the verdant **Cuckmere Valley**; secluded forest; and, finally, the undulating chalky cliffs of the **Seven Sisters** and **Beachy Head**.

To Southease and the downs

5.5km

If you are starting this walk from Southease station, exit the station from the same side that the Lewes train deposited you on, then see the bolded mention of the station in the paragraph below.

To rejoin the South Downs Way from Telscombe, leave the village as you came, remembering to turn left into the field through the metal gate after 250m rather than continuing on the road (though both will take you to Southease). Once you reach the farm, simply follow the track straight ahead rather than ascending the downs. At the end of the gravel track, turn right, following the wooden signpost; a grassy path leads up the hill towards the road. Turn left on the little road, then cross the main road and follow the signs to the left to **Southease**.

This small and extremely pretty settlement is distinguished by a round-towered **Saxon church**. Inside are faint traces of thirteenth-century wall paintings depicting scenes from the life of Christ. From the church, follow the minor road which leads straight through the village and over the River Ouse. At the **station**, cross the railway line, through the gates. A track leads up to Itford Farm and the busy A26; cross the road and turn right, then left almost immediately, onto the South Downs Way. From here you start the steady, steep ascent of the downs, until you reach the top of the ridge, with good views north to **Mount Caburn** (see p.76).

Along the downs to Alfriston

10km

For the next 10km, the path sweeps along the top of the downs. Despite the views of Newhaven to the south and Lewes to the north, you get a real sense of quiet and isolation here. Apart from the radio mast ahead, the other features you'll notice on this stretch are the tumuli which lie to either side of the path. These rounded grassy burial mounds are **Bronze Age barrows** – the largest would originally have stood up to 6m high, but all have been eroded over the centuries and opened either by thieves or antiquarians. The barrows were built by a people known as the **Beaker Folk**,

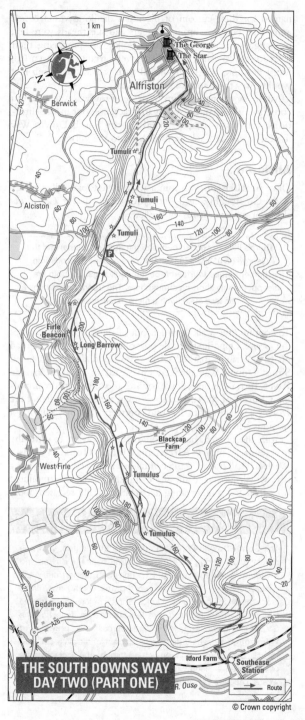

THE SOUTH DOWNS WAY
DAY TWO (PART ONE)

© Crown copyright

named for their custom of placing a drinking vessel beside entombed bodies – bronze daggers and spearheads were left, too, suggesting that the Beaker Folk were preparing their dead for the afterlife. The bodies were arranged in a curled, foetal position, as if the rounded barrow was the womb that would carry them into the next world.

Eventually the path begins to descend towards Alfriston. You come to a **crossroads**, with paths radiating out in five directions. Carry on straight ahead on the South Downs Way itself. The chalky track drops down into the village.

Alfriston

Once in **Alfriston**, you join a wide tarred road called King's Ride. Go straight ahead until you see the Tudor *George Inn* ahead of you; the *Star* is on the left.

There's little to choose between the *Star* (no phone) and the *George* (℡ 01323/870319). Both are housed in handsome timber-framed fourteenth-century buildings, but both are disappointingly short on atmosphere. The *George* is perhaps a little less staid, with a more extensive menu.

To continue the walk, turn left out of the *Star* or right out of the *George*. Opposite the little post office building there's a road off to the right, marked with a dead-end sign and a faded South Downs Way marker. This leads to the **Cuckmere River**. Turn right here, down towards the unexpectedly imposing **Church of St Andrews** – known as the "Cathedral of the Downs", it dates from the mid-fourteenth century and has a spacious cruciform interior.

From the church, head through the graveyard towards the fourteenth-century **Alfriston Clergy House**. This is a Wealden "hall house" – the central hall is flanked by two-storey bays which jut out to the front, and the whole is surmounted by a thatched roof, creating a characteristically recessed door-

Shorter route to Eastbourne

The **South Downs Way** splits into two at Alfriston, with one route (10km) taking you to Eastbourne over the downs and avoiding the spectacular but testing (and longer) cliff walk described below. To join this branch of the South Downs Way, cross the bridge over the Cuckmere shortly before you reach the Church of St Andrew and turn left after 100m, following the South Downs Way signs. After 2km you pass the **Long Man of Wilmington**, a seventy-metre-high ancient chalk giant cut onto the hill. Some 3km further on you go through the ancient village of **Jevington**, beyond which the route descends for 5km to the western edge of **Eastbourne**.

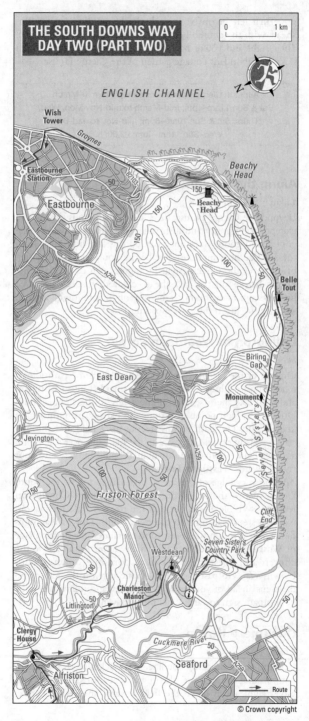

THE SOUTH DOWNS WAY
DAY TWO (PART TWO)

0   1 km

ENGLISH CHANNEL

Wish Tower

Groynes

Eastbourne Station

Beachy Head

150
Beachy Head

Eastbourne

50

B2103

150

150

100

A259

50

Belle Tout

East Dean

Birling Gap

Monument

100

50

Seven Sisters

Jevington

100

50

150

Friston Forest

Cliff End

Westdean

Seven Sisters Country Park

Charleston Manor

50

Litlington

Clergy House

50

Cuckmere River

50

Seaford

A259

Alfriston

Route

© Crown copyright

way. Turn left before you reach the house, then go straight ahead, with the church behind you, through the squeeze gate. Turn right and you're back on the bank of the river, which skirts the abundant cottage garden of the Clergy House.

**Alfriston Clergy House is open early to mid-March
Sat & Sun 11am–4pm; mid-March to mid-Nov Mon, Wed,
Thurs, Sat & Sun 10am–5pm; mid-Nov to mid-Dec
Wed–Sun 11am–4pm; £2.80; NT.**

Along the Cuckmere

1.5km

Beyond the Clergy House, the **Cuckmere** winds through an exceptionally pretty and lush valley – it's hard to believe that contraband goods were once run up this lazy little river from the sea (see box opposite). Just before you reach the wooden bridge over the Cuckmere at Litlington, you can see a white **chalk horse** on the hill ahead, created in 1924 by three brothers who cut the horse by moonlight one night so as to surprise the locals the next morning.

Litlington to Westdean Forest

3km

Once over the bridge, turn right. After 150m the path joins a road opposite a huge thatched house; turn left into **Litlington** and then take the first right. Immediately to the right, a South Downs Way sign points you onto the narrow path, through a kissing gate. The path climbs steeply up a field and through another kissing gate. Carry on up the field and over a stile into another field – then head downhill, keeping the fence to your right, towards **Westdean Forest**.

At the very edge of the forest, turn left to follow the South Downs Way – the handsome thirteenth-century **Charleston Manor** is visible ahead through the trees. A little further on, wooden steps lead up into the trees. South Downs Way signs direct you through the forest to the secluded medieval village of **Westdean**. Ignore the road which curves round left to the church and go straight ahead to continue on the South Downs Way. Go past the green phone box on the left, climb the steps ahead of you through the trees, and follow the public footpath sign towards Cuckmere Haven.

Cuckmere Haven

2.5km

Coming out of the forest you'll see the Cuckmere river ahead of you, snaking through the silted estuary at **Cuckmere Haven**. Go straight ahead down the field towards the visitor centre.

Jevington Jigg and the Sussex gentlemen

Five and twenty ponies
Trotting through the dark –
Brandy for the Parson,
'Baccy for the Clerk;
Laces for a lady, letters for a spy,
And watch the wall, my darling, while the Gentlemen go by!

Rudyard Kipling, *The Smugglers Song*

Smuggling has a very long history in Sussex – wool-running, known as "owling", started in the thirteenth century following the imposition of a severe tax on wool under Edward I, and continued into the eighteenth century. By this time, smuggling had developed into a serious industry, with goods, from brandy to lace and tea, being smuggled in from the continent.

Kipling's use of the word "gentlemen" to describe the smugglers was not entirely ironic. Many gangs of smugglers were bankrolled by City of London financiers, and whole villages, from estate owners to innkeepers, were involved. One such innkeeper was James Pettit, known as **Jevington Jigg**, who operated out of the *Eight Bells* in Jevington, running contraband from Birling Gap. Jevington Jigg was a kind of Sussex Ned Kelly, though with fewer principles, and led a lawless and incident-packed life – when once trapped in an inn surrounded by armed constables, he managed to escape by slipping into a petticoat and feigning girlish hysterics. In 1789 he was arrested with his friend Cream Pot Tom for stealing a mare in Firle. Tom was hanged at Oxford, but Jevington Jigg was released, leading people to suspect he had betrayed his friend. He was later nearly lynched at Lewes for informing on other associates. Eventually Jevington Jigg's luck ran out: he was convicted of horse theft and transported to Botany Bay in Australia, and probably died there.

Today the exploits of the smugglers, including a small gang which operated out of Alfriston, are much romanticized, despite their violent and sometimes murderous treatment of excise men. Traces of tunnels beneath inns and manor houses – and even the church in Jevington – built to hide contraband goods from the excise men, are their last reminder of the trade.

Across the busy road and over the cattle grid, the path splits, the South Downs Way climbing high up the valley wall and a second track leading beside the river. If you want to save yourself a strenuous climb, it's quite possible to follow the track along the river, picking up the South Downs Way slightly over a kilometre further on – you can make a little detour on to the beach from the lower path.

The track and the other paths join and then diverge once more; the South Downs Way follows the steeper route to the left, taking you onto the downs again.

The Seven Sisters, Birling Gap and Beachy Head

7km

From here on you need to brace yourself for the dramatic walk over the switchback sequence of cliffs known as the **Seven Sisters**. The path runs close to the edge of the chalky cliffs, with the only break in the clifftop walk being provided by **Birling Gap**, a small settlement featuring a row of nineteenth-century coastguards' cottages. Beyond, the clifftop walk takes you on a further rollercoaster ride to **Beachy Head**, the highest point of the cliffs (160m). The wildness of the surroundings helps to explain why Debussy came here to complete *La Mer*, his masterly evocation of the sea; he stayed at the Grand Hotel on the front in nearby Eastbourne. Look out for the red and white candy stripes of the glorious **lighthouse**, built in 1902, just off the coast at Beachy Head.

Into Eastbourne

5km

At the *Beachy Head* pub just to the left of the route, you begin to descend into Eastbourne. Take the tarred path which leads off to the right, via a viewpoint. Cross the metal gate and descend the narrow wooded path for 1.5km. Below you is **Eastbourne**, whose Edwardian villas can look unexpectedly glamorous in the evening light. The last gasp of downland walk takes you down a steep grassy slope, and lands you right on Eastbourne's seafront.

Follow the seafront for just over 1.5km, heading towards the pier; turn left onto Terminus Road for the **station**. If you're flagging at this point, a **taxi** (℡01323/725511) to the station from the seafront will cost around £4.

4

The Saxon Shore

L eading along the coast from Hastings in Sussex to Gravesend in Kent, the **Saxon Shore Way** is named for the string of late-Roman fortifications which protected the coast against Saxon invasion, and whose remains you can still see today, as at Anderida, which features on the second walk in this chapter. The stretch of Sussex shoreline covered in this chapter has always been particularly vulnerable to invasion; indeed, it was at Anderida that William the Conqueror landed – the 1066 Country Walk follows the route of his army inland to Battle.

The **levels** are the defining physical feature of the first two walks in this chapter: a landscape of fields and banks, reclaimed from the sea and crisscrossed by little man-made channels (known, rather off-puttingly, as "sewers"). Reclamation was an expensive and therefore very gradual process, begun by the Romans, revived in the eighth century by monastic houses which owned tracts of marshland, and continued into the eighteenth century. The result of this piecemeal development is an idiosyncratic landscape of small and irregularly shaped fields, scattered with shells which offer a reminder of the land's watery origins. The marshy, reed-fringed **peninsula** near which Fishbourne Palace sits offers a reminder of how the levels must have looked before they were reclaimed.

The first walk leads along part of the **Saxon Shore Way**, starting with a strenuous hike along the cliffs at Hastings, then descending to cross the Pett Levels and reach the lovely little town of Winchelsea. The second (and longest) walk, the **1066 Country Walk**, takes you along the route followed by the Normans from their landing place at Pevensey, across the Pevensey Levels and through wooded hills to Battle. This is designed as a two-day walk, but with enough energy and an early start, you could do it in one day. Finally, the **Chichester Harbour** walk leads from Fishbourne Palace, with its fine Roman mosaics, through marshland and pasture to the appealing village of Bosham.

Train journeys to reach these destinations are on the long side (1hr 20min–1hr 40min), but with all these walks you don't need to **start walking** until around 11.30am. (The only exception is if you plan to do the 1066 walk in one day instead of two, in which case it will take you seven to eight hours.) Trains leave from **Charing Cross** for Hastings on the Saxon Shore Way, with stops at Waterloo and London Bridge. For the 1066 Country Walk take the train to Pevensey and Westham from **Victoria**, which also stops at Clapham Junction. For the Chichester Harbour walk, trains leave from **Waterloo**, stopping at Clapham Junction. The easiest walk for **drivers** is the circular Chichester Harbour one.

The Saxon Shore Way

Hastings to Winchelsea, via Cliff End

Distance and difficulty: 17km; strenuous.
Train: London Charing Cross to Hastings (every 30min; 1hr 20min); return from Winchelsea to Hastings (hourly; 15min), then Hastings to London Charing Cross (every 30min; 1hr 20min).
Map: OS Landranger 199 and 189: *Eastbourne & Hastings* and *Ashford & Romney Marsh*; OS Explorer 124: *Hastings & Bexhill*.

This glorious walk is very much a day of two halves, starting as a strenuous stomp along the clifftops near Hastings before descending to the pancake-flat "levels" beyond. The route follows part of the **Saxon Shore Way**, a long-distance path which runs for 260km in its entirety, from Hastings all the way round the coast to Gravesend. Starting in tattily charismatic **Hastings**, a dinky funicular whisks you up to the blustery sandstone cliffs that soar above the town into the pristine downland of the **Hastings Country Park**. From here, the route follows the clifftops for 5km, taking in sweeping sea views and dipping down into luxuriant wooded glens before terminating at the prosaically named village of **Cliff End**; a short detour leads from here to a long sandy **beach**, where it's sometimes safe to swim. From Cliff End, the walk runs across **Pett Level**, reclaimed from the sea and crisscrossed by water channels. Though the scenery is less obviously dramatic than along the clifftop walk, the levels have an enticingly still atmosphere and are prettily framed by hills to the north and the long bank of the sea wall to the south. The walk ends at **Winchelsea**, an attractive little town with a fascinating history.

The Saxon Shore Way is irregularly **signed** – waymarkers show a red circle with a horned helmet, the horns pointing in the relevant direction. There are lots of wonderful **picnic** spots along the way, but you may want to detour to the excellent *Two Sawyers* at Pett for **lunch**. It's cheapest and quickest to return from Winchelsea via Hastings, meaning that you can buy a return ticket to Hastings. Alternatively, infrequent trains run from Winchelsea to London **via Ashford**, but if you go for this option you have to buy two single tickets rather than a return.

Getting started

2km

From **Hastings station**, go straight ahead down Havelock Road, then straight ahead down Wellington Place, through a

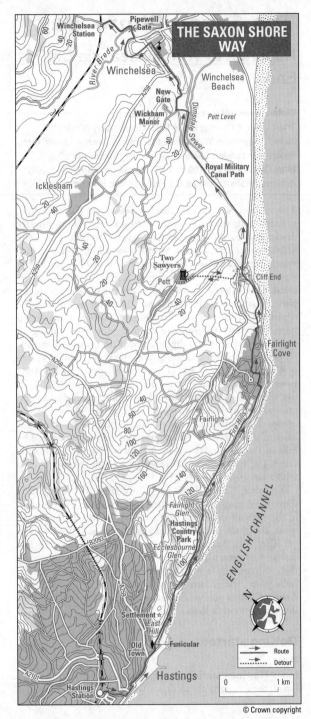

pedestrian underpass and towards the old town. Turn left along the sea front and continue for 700m, past Hastings' appealingly shabby jumble of Regency and Victorian buildings, amusement arcades and fish 'n' chip shops. Where the road curves left, cross over onto the side road and follow the signs towards Underwater World. This picturesque part of town is known as the **Stade**, from the old English for "landing place" – Hastings still has a working fleet, and you'll see brightly coloured boats on the shingle, amongst the unusually tall black wooden fishing huts which lend the area a quirky Gothic air. These were built in the nineteenth century to store nets and ropes – as the sea came in much further at that time, fishermen were forced to capitalize on the available space by building up rather than out.

Hastings Country Park

5km

Opposite the cluster of fishing huts, the East Hill **funicular railway**, Britain's steepest at 39 degrees, runs up the cliff side at surprising speed (April–Sept 10am–5.30pm; Oct & Nov 11am–4pm; 90p). If you want to start walking before the funicular starts running, or if it's poorly, which happens from time to time, you'll have to climb the cliff via Tamarisk Steps to the left of the train tracks. The funicular provides tremendous views of the town, and lands you neatly in **Hastings Country Park**, whose cliffs tower up to 90m above the sea and are aflame with yellow gorse in the summer. You pick up the Saxon Shore Way here, though it's not signed; follow the brown signs towards Firehills. If in doubt at any point in the park, head for the path closest to the cliffs.

Go straight ahead and up the hill past the Pitch and Putt hut. The hill is surmounted by a low, circular-banked structure, the remains of an **Iron Age fort**. The views are tremendous, with the sea to the right, Hastings to the left and the cliffs you'll walk along ahead. Just beyond the fort, head right to the long wooden fence that runs along a field. From here, simply follow the path as it hugs the cliff edge and dips down into first **Ecclesbourne** and then **Fairlight Glen**, two wooded clefts in the cliffs, following the brown signs to Fairlight and/or Firehills. There's a nudist beach at Fairlight, although the council recommends that you avoid it because of recent cliff falls – even so, there always seem to be a few hopeful teenage boys keeping a lookout on the cliffs just in case. Coming out of Fairlight Glen, follow the wide grassy path that leads up the hill and briefly veers left, away from the cliffs, then follow the signs to Fairlight Church and Firehills. Some 400m beyond here you'll pass a radio mast on top of the hill; carry on straight ahead to Firehills on the path to the right, not the one that leads inland.

Fairlight to Cliff End

3km

From the country park, you emerge into staid **Fairlight**. Go straight ahead along Channel Way, a track that leads between the rows of bungalows and the sea. Because of cliff erosion on the far side of Channel Way, part of the path is closed and you have to make a rather tedious detour through the houses. Some 500m along Channel Way, turn left onto Shepherd's Way, and after 100m turn right onto Bramble Way. After 250m turn left onto Smuggler's Way then, after 200m, take a right onto Lower Wait's Lane (also signed Fairlight Gardens). This lane cuts through the village for 750m. At the junction ahead, turn right. About 100m further on you'll see a National Trust sign. Go through the gap in the hedge here, onto the path which leads through a field, and climbs away from Fairlight. You'll soon see a fence post with a Saxon Shore Way sign.

The cliff-top walk resumes from this point. Out of the National Trust area, follow the yellow arrow on the fence post – you'll see a gorgeous golden strand ahead. You're now in **Cliff End**. Head down the hill for 400m, past two pretty thatched cottages – ignore the turn-offs and go straight ahead downhill until you get to the road. Turn right and keep going for 300m to get to the **beach**, but don't swim if the red flag is flying.

If you want to detour (2km) to the pub in Pett, turn left at the point where the Saxon Shore Way joins the road through Cliff End. After 50m you'll see a public footpath sign on the right pointing into a field. Cross the field and then turn right uphill by the orange cottage for 700m until you emerge in Pett, where you'll find the *Two Saywers* pub (℡ 01424/812255), a rambling old beamed building with a nice shady back garden. The pub serves good simple pub food and has its own beer, Pett Progress, plus seasonal guest beers. To rejoin the walk, return to Cliff End the way you came.

Pett Levels

4km

To continue along the Saxon Shore Way, turn right at the point where the path joins the road through Cliff End and head towards the beach. After 100m, where the road curves, take the path to the left along the **Royal Military Canal**, built by William Pitt for defence against a Napoleonic invasion which never materialized. After 200m you come to a little bridge – don't cross over here, but go straight ahead up the left bank of the canal, on a narrow and slightly scruffy path. After another 200m you'll see a brick pillbox on the left

– just before you reach it, turn right over a second bridge to cross the canal. (The official signposted route continues on the left bank here and crosses at the third bridge, but the path can be very overgrown so it's better to cross here.) Continue up the right bank of the canal. At a third bridge, cross the road and carry on up the canal.

From here you're on **Pett Level** proper and the views open up – the canal heads gradually away from the sea and the noisy seafront road, drawing closer to the hills to the north, where you'll see a windmill. At a kink in the canal the Dimsdale Sewer (actually a water channel, so not as unappetizing as it sounds) appears on your right, so you're walking between the two stretches of water. Where the canal curves to the right there's a bridge – don't cross over here, but continue for another 700m until you begin to draw near to a white clapboard house away to the left.

Cross at the **concrete bridge** here, marked with yellow public footpath arrows. Go straight ahead across the field towards the road, then follow the curve of the track up the hill to the left. Cross the stile and turn right onto a minor road. After 100m you come to **New Gate**, one of the medieval entrances to Winchelsea. Go through New Gate then look back and you'll see that the arch of the gate perfectly frames **Wickham Manor**, a fine early sixteenth-century farmhouse. Follow the road for 700m into Winchelsea.

Winchelsea

3km

On your right as you enter the main part of town is the great **Church of St Thomas**. The transepts and nave were entirely destroyed by the French, so that the remaining part, the chancel, feels bizarrely abbreviated. Its scale, however, is still grand and the detail splendidly ornate. To either side are sombre fourteenth-century effigies – two depict admirals of the Cinque Ports, and the others are generic, representing a knight, a lady and a civilian. The 1920s stained glass adds splashes of colour, but its close leading doesn't allow for much expression.

Opposite the church is the *New Inn*, a scenic spot for a pint, and nearby is a scion of **Wesley's Tree**; John Wesley frequently preached at Winchelsea and delivered his last sermon, against smuggling, under the original tree in 1790. The town mainly consists of well-proportioned sixteenth- to eighteenth-century town houses, with some harmonious early twentieth-century imitations. The only surviving medieval building-work, apart from the much-damaged church, is in the wine cellars concealed beneath many of the houses.

From the church, go straight ahead for 150m until you come to a post with a **1066 sign** pointing to the left. You can

Winchelsea: storms, smuggling and sacking

The pretty and now rather sedate town of **Winchelsea** was shaped over the centuries both by natural disasters and by brutal attacks. The town originally sat on a long shingle spit that poked out into the sea from Fairlight cliffs. By the thirteenth century, however, the spit was being eaten away by erosion. A huge **storm** in 1252 and a freak high tide swallowed up three hundred houses, while another storm in 1288 converted the spit into an island. It was decided to move Winchelsea to higher and safer ground – the remains of the old town are now completely submerged, and even their exact whereabouts are unknown.

Edward I employed a French architect, who designed the town along the lines of a French *bastide* (fortified town) on a neat grid plan that survives today. The town was built primarily for commerce, and was a vital link in the wine trade with Bordeaux, as well as being a place from where fish, wool, cheese and salt were exported, plus iron and wool from the Weald. There was a good road to London, and each merchant was given wharf space on the River Brede, which was then wide and flourishing. The king imposed a perpetual rent on the town in return for the building costs, and a sum of just over £14 – a figure which has remained unchanged through the centuries – is still collected annually.

Prior to the rebuilding, the strategic significance of Winchelsea had already been recognized by its inclusion in the **Cinq Ports** confederation. This was a grouping of five towns – Hastings, New Romney, Hythe, Sandwich and Dover – to which Winchelsea and Rye were later added. At a time when Britain had no navy, the Cinq Ports were the only line of defence against a possible invasion of southern England. In exchange for providing ships and men for a certain number of days a year, the ports were granted freedom from taxation and the governance of their own affairs. This arrangement was open to abuse, however: Winchelsea carried on a lively trade in the **smuggling** of tax-free goods, and also engaged in piracy – its sailors were notorious for preying on English and foreign ships.

The town's wealth and strategic location made it vulnerable to **attack**. In 1359, while the inhabitants were at Mass, the French stormed Winchelsea, killing forty people and burning and looting the town. They returned exactly a year later, and again in 1380 and 1449, on similarly violent missions. But it was natural forces that were to prove the undoing of Winchelsea. Early in the sixteenth century, great masses of shingle from the Channel caused the River Brede to silt up and narrow. The town's days as a port were finished.

Following the silting up of the river, Winchelsea went into economic decline for more than three centuries, the gaps in its grid

continued opposite

of streets caused by the French leading both Daniel Defoe and John Wesley to liken the place to a skeleton. This melancholy shade of a town began to draw writers and artists from the end of the nineteenth century: Turner and Millais painted here; Henry James, Thackeray, Conrad, Ford Madox Ford, Rumer Godden and Radclyffe Hall were visitors; and the actress Ellen Terry lived in Tower Cottage at the north end of town. Although they were attracted by Winchelsea's air of romantic decay, their presence in the town undoubtedly contributed to its transformation into the prosperous little place you see today.

avoid walking on the main road by following the 1066 sign for 900m, and there are fine views across the marshes – this was a lookout point during the medieval wars with the French. Cross the main road and go straight ahead, following the 1066 Country Walk signs which lead you in a loop down to the minor road that runs to the station. Otherwise, turn right down the main road, through Pipewell Gate. At the hairpin bend, follow the minor road signed towards the station, which zigzags for a kilometre to **Winchelsea station**, from where trains depart to Hastings (hourly; 15min) or on to London Charing Cross via Ashford (every 30min; 2hr).

The 1066 Country Walk

Pevensey to Battle via Brownbread Street

Distance and difficulty: day 1: 17.5km; day 2: 12.5km; moderate.
Train: London Victoria to Pevensey and Westham (every 30min; 1hr 40min); return from Battle to London Bridge (every 30min; 1hr 10min).
Map: OS Landranger 199: *Eastbourne & Hastings*; OS Explorer 124: *Hasting & Bexhill*.

This wonderfully varied two-day walk is part of the **1066 Country Walk**, which follows the route taken by the Norman army from Pevensey, where they landed and established a castle within the walls of a Roman fort, to Battle, where they defeated King Harold's army (the official route then continues for another 28km through Winchelsea to Rye). Starting in **Pevensey**, then curving through the flat and watery **Pevensey Levels** and across rolling wooded hills to the imposing abbey at **Battle**, the walk brings this well-worn piece of English history vividly to life. There are many incidental pleasures along the way, from the sight of herons slowly rising above the Pevensey Levels to the reconstructed Elizabethan castle and bizarrely attractive observatory at **Herstmonceux**, as well as the pretty hamlets you pass on the second day's walk.

It's possible to do just the first day of this walk, taking a taxi from Boreham Street to Battle. Alternatively, considering the whole route isn't hugely long, and providing you get an early start, it's also possible to walk the whole way from Pevensey to Battle in one day. The walk is very easy to follow – just look for the circular red **1066 signs**, whose stylized Norman arrows point you in the right direction.

Day one

17.5km

Day one starts at **Pevensey and Westham station** – a little further down the line there's a station simply called Pevensey which is slightly closer to the castle and the start of the walk proper, but trains don't run there at weekends. **Pevensey** was the landing place of Duke William of Normandy (although the sea has receded, leaving the town high and dry), who established himself in the great circular Roman fort of Anderida – the ruins of the Roman fort and the Norman

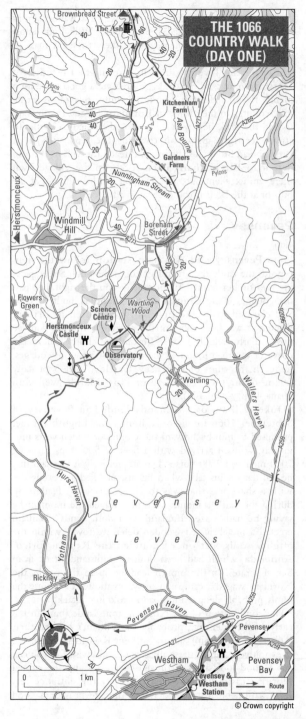

THE 1066
COUNTRY WALK
(DAY ONE)

Brownbread Street

The Ash

Kitchenham Farm

Ash Bourne

Gardners Farm

Nunningham Stream

Windmill Hill

Boreham Street

Wartling Wood

Flowers Green

Science Centre

Herstmonceux Castle

Observatory

Wartling

Wallers Haven

Herstmonceux

Hurst Haven

P e v e n s e y

L e v e l s

Yotham

Rickney

Pevensey Haven

Pevensey

Westham

Pevensey Bay

Pevensey & Westham Station

0   1 km

→ Route

© Crown copyright

castle constructed within it are well worth a wander. From the castle, the well-marked 1066 Country Walk leads across the Pevensey Levels, where you're likely to see a mass of water birds.

Leaving the levels you climb uphill to the edge of **Herstmonceux**, whose castle grounds are a good place for a picnic. Beyond Herstmonceux, the route runs across fertile hilly country to the village of **Boreham Street**. If you want to end the walk here, you'll have to take a taxi to Battle. To stay overnight, press on towards the tiny village of Brownbread Street. Just before you reach the village you can detour to **Kitchenham Farm** B&B. In the village itself there's an excellent pub, *The Ash*; you can have dinner at the pub, or at the B&B if you order it in advance.

Pevensey

1km

From **Pevensey and Westham station**, follow the signs towards the castle then turn right onto the High Street, passing two timber-framed Tudor cottages on the right. Just past the cottages is the **Church of St Nicholas**, built in 1080 and claimed to be the first Norman church in Britain, though it was later substantially altered, and what you see now is Early English in style. Beyond the church, follow the curve of the road round to the right, past a row of cottages, to reach the ruins of **Pevensey Castle** (April–Sept daily 10am–6pm; Oct 10am–5pm; Nov–March Wed–Sun 10am–4pm; £2.80; EH).

Duke William of Normandy landed in Pevensey in September 1066 intent on claiming the English throne, promised to him by Edward the Confessor fifteen years previously. William arrived with a fleet of 500 ships carrying 7000 men and 2500 horses. Less impressively, it was said that he fell flat on his face when he disembarked at Pevensey – with a sharpness that was to characterize his leadership during the battle a month later, he salvaged the moment by saying he had "seized England with both hands". William erected a prefabricated wooden defensive tower within the mighty walls that once encircled the Roman fort of **Anderida**, which had been built to withstand attack from Saxon pirates. In the month leading up to the battle, the Normans waged a campaign of systematic terror against the locals, probably designed to goad Harold into attack.

The combination of the Norman stone castle (built in the early twelfth century, probably by William's half-brother, Robert of Mortmain) and the ancient Roman walls provide as evocative a start to the walk as you could wish for; you can get a good look at both the Roman walls and the ruined Norman castle without having to pay the entrance fee. Information boards erected round the site provide a good context for what you're looking at, and include a representation of a panel of the Bayeux tapestry, on which the name "Pevensae" can be clearly seen.

From the castle, go back past the row of cottages and turn right, following the road as it curves round past the rugged outer walls of the castle – from here you can see a couple of pillboxes, constructed in concealed positions in the walls in 1940 in response to the threat of German invasion.

Pevensey Levels

6km

After 600m, follow the first **1066 sign** to the left, down a narrow and often muddy path. After 250m, the path comes to the thunderous A259 – cross the road and follow the path as it resumes on the other side, running along the left bank of **Pevensey Haven**, one of the many channels cut to drain the levels. This first part of the walk is a little uninspiring, especially as you can hear the noise of the road for a while, but things soon pick up, and you should begin to spot some of the abundant birdlife: herons, ducks redshanks, warblers, swans, grebes and sandpipers. Plants line the havens, including great reed mace and yellow water iris.

The path follows the gentle curve of the haven for 3km to the quiet hamlet of **Rickney**. Here the 1066 route splits into two – follow the sign to Battle through the village, crossing a bridge over a little stream. From this point the character of the **Pevensey Levels**, framed by the South Downs to the south and wooded hills to the north, is much more apparent: a network of streams and ditches reflect the light, and herons and swans can be seen in profusion. The path runs for 3km through a series of gates, along the right bank of the wide and fast-flowing haven. Alongside the pedestrian gates which dot the route you'll see wider farm gates and, between them, horse jumps – this is very horsey country, and you're likely to see a few riders out and about.

Towards Herstmonceux

1km

A couple of kilometres ahead is the green dome of Herstmonceux observatory, which you pass later in the day, and the spire of the church at **Herstmonceux** – the name is a combination of the Saxon *herst*, meaning forest, and de Monceux, the name of the Conqueror's grandson, though it's now pronounced in a resolutely English fashion as "Herst-mont-zoo".

Keep your eyes peeled for the 1066 sign and follow it away from the haven to the right (there's another post with a 1066 sign just beyond to confirm that you're on correct path). The path curves round to the left, over a stile, and then turns into a broad, grassy track, running between two ditches. Head up towards the church – the path climbs up the hill through a field, with a fence to your left. At the top of the field, turn right to go along the field, with the church on your left. Cross through the gap in the fence towards the church, follow the path round the churchyard, then go over the stile into the churchyard.

Looking out over the Pevensey Levels from the southeast fringes of Herstmonceux village, **All Saints Church** was built around a century after the Conquest, although the dormer windows – which give the long nave roof a rather gingerbread-cottage look – were a Victorian addition, designed to bring more light to the interior. Inside, look out for the sturdy medieval trussed roof and the long brass on the chancel floor (it may be concealed by a carpet) depicting Sir William Fiennes and dating from 1402 – he wears a mail shirt and sword and his pointy feet rest on a lion. The Gothic **Dacre Chapel** to the left of the altar was built with funds provided in 1534 by the Dacre family, who were then living at Herstmonceux Castle (see below). The chapel shelters an unusual double effigy, restored in brilliant colour, which commemorates Thomas, the eighth Lord Dacre (1470–1533), his feet resting on a bull representing the Dacres, and his son, Sir Thomas Fiennes, whose feet are supported by a wolfhound, the symbol of the Fiennes family (now of handsome actor and explorer fame). It's thought that the carving originally represented a pair of half-brothers, but was brought from Battle Abbey following the dissolution of the monasteries and adapted to represent Lord Dacre and Sir Thomas.

Herstmonceux to Boreham Street

3km

From the church, you can head left down the road to the main part of **Herstmonceux village** if you want to make a detour for a pub lunch; of the two options in the village, the *Brewer's Arms* is definitely the best, though it's not really worth the three-kilometre detour.

To continue the walk from the church, go straight ahead across the road from the stile by the churchyard and follow the 1066 sign towards Herstmonceux Castle. The path goes downhill through some pine woods before emerging into an open field. From here, you can see the green dome of the observatory looming ahead of you and **Herstmonceux Castle** to the left – a bizarre juxtaposition, resembling the backdrop to one of Tintin's more outré adventures. The beautifully symmetrical castle, really more of a manor house, was amongst the earliest brick structures in England. It was built by Sir Roger Fiennes, who obtained the necessary "licence to crenellate" in 1440, but fell into disuse and disrepair and was dismantled in 1777, before being reconstructed in 1932 by Sir Paul Latham. In 1946 the estate was purchased by the Admiralty as a home for the Royal Observatory, and in 1993 both the observatory and castle were purchased by a Canadian university.

Head towards the **observatory**, up the steepish stepped path through some woodland. On the left at the top of the hill you'll see smaller steel and copper domes belonging to the Herstmonceux Science Centre; the place is now run as an education facility rather than a serious observatory (the main telescope was shifted in the 1980s to the Canary Islands, where the weather is obviously more reliable). The path goes straight ahead through beech and pine wood, then joins a minor road. Turn right onto the road for 200m, then left just before the orange-tiled cottage.

The path runs down the edge of a field, with Wartling Wood on the left, then climbs up a field and curves to join another minor road. Turn right on the road and then almost immediately left over a stile into a field, then cross a series of stiles over paddock fences as you head diagonally across the field towards a black barn. The path then curves left towards a line of trees – cross the stile on the far side of field, from where you'll see a farm and some houses, and go straight ahead then left round the edge of the field towards the houses and road. Cross the stile leading onto the road on the right, just before you get to the barn. Head down to the road and turn right into **Boreham Street**, an attractive village with some fine Georgian houses and cottages.

If you want to end the walk here, a taxi (Battle Taxis ☎ 01424/777 2222) to Battle station will cost about £8.

Towards Brownbread Street

4.5km

Just outside Boreham Street, a 1066 sign points left to Brownbread Street – the path heads very steeply down a field, with superb views ahead made more dramatic by the line of giant pylons that marches across it. At the bottom of the hill you come to a stream; cross this and carry straight on up the hill, following the 1066 sign, past **Gardners Farm**, where the path becomes a farm track. A kilometre beyond the farm the track joins a minor road. Go right and continue for another kilometre to come out at a grassy triangle with a red-brick house on the right-hand side. The route to **Kitchenham Farm** B&B (see p.108) leads off to the right from here. The friendly owner of the B&B will either pick you up from the pub or give you a lift there and back from the farm.

To reach the **Ash Tree Inn** turn left and follow the sign to **Brownbread Street** for 200m – the inn is a free house and makes an excellent stop for an evening meal and a pint, with outside tables in a pretty garden.

To Kitchenham Farm

2km

To get to the B&B, turn right instead of left at the red-brick house. After 100m you'll see a wide metal gate on the right with a public footpath sign and stile. Cross the stile and follow the footpath downhill, keeping the patch of woodland to the left, then curve round the field to the right and through the gap in the trees soon after. Continue heading downhill, following the line of the hedge to the right, towards the pylon and the orange-tiled cottage – to the right of the cottage on top of the low hill ahead of you is **Kitchenham Farm** itself, with an oast house next to it. Cross the stile, following the public footpath sign, across the marshy field, then go across the concrete bridge over the Ash Bourne, through the metal gate and up the hill past the cottage. At the top of the hill, turn right and walk through the farm buildings to reach the B&B.

....

Kitchenham Farm (Ⓣ01424/892221, Ⓕ893618, Ⓦwwwrye.uk.co/kitchenham) is fine-looking farmhouse, built in 1750 and surrounded by picturesque outbuildings. It's a working farm, mainly arable, and the house is very much a family home. There's one en-suite double room (£50) and two twins (with shower £50; shared shower £45) – the rooms are prettily furnished without being twee, and extremely comfortable. Dinner, which should be ordered in advance, costs £10–15; the cooked breakfast, included in the room rate, is substantial and tasty.

....

Day two

12.5km

On **day two** of the walk, paths and minor roads lead through verdant, undulating countryside, punctuated by small settlements such as **Ashburnham Forge** and **Steven's Crouch**. You should reach Battle in time for lunch on day two – if you don't, there are several shops and pubs along the way, so you won't go hungry. Eventually the walk runs uphill, skirting the site of the most momentous battle in English history, and lands you at the fine fortified gatehouse of **Battle Abbey**.

Back to Brownbread Street

2km

The beginning of the day's walk involves retracing your steps (assuming you walked, and didn't catch a lift) back towards Brownbread Street. Exit Kitchenham Farm past the oast house on the right, then follow the track downhill between the farm buildings and the road, back the way you came.

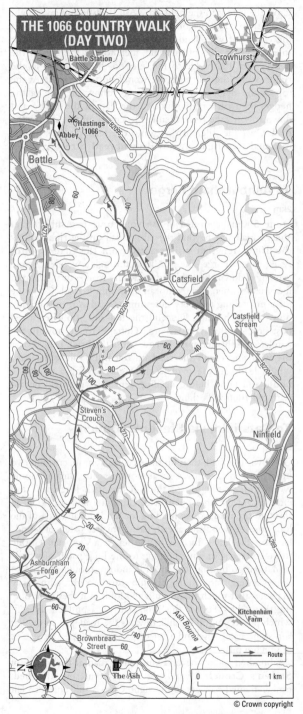

THE 1066 COUNTRY WALK
(DAY TWO)

Crowhurst

Battle Station

Hastings
1066

Abbey

Battle

Catsfield

Catsfield
Stream

Steven's
Crouch

Ninfield

Ashburnham
Forge

Kitchenham
Farm

Brownbread
Street

Ash Bourne

The Ash

Route

0   1 km

© Crown copyright

Cross the gate into the field, cross Ash Bourne and go straight ahead, then curve diagonally across the field, heading towards the clump of woodland on the hill to the right. Cross the stile at the far side of the field, then follow the line of the hedge, with the hedge to the left and the big pylon to the right. Go up the hill, with the woodland to the right. At the top of the field, turn left briefly to follow the line of the hedge, then turn right through the gap in the hedge and down towards the trees, then left to climb up the field to the road. Over the stile, turn left onto the road, go back up the road and turn right towards **Brownbread Street**, past *The Ash*.

To Ashburnham Forge

2km

Some 500m beyond *The Ash* you come to Ashburnham Village Hall; just beyond the village hall on the right, follow the 1066 sign that points away from the road towards Ashburnham Forge. The path leads through a wooden kissing gate, then down the field and on to the road – turn left for a few metres, then right onto another minor road. Continue for a mile along this very quiet minor road as it rolls up and down through fields. Descend the hill and you'll see a red post box; on the right is Forge Cottage. You're now in the hamlet of **Ashburnham Forge**. Cross the brick bridge over the weir and climb the road up the hill. Follow the path which leads off the road to the right, passing a red-brick house and pond before heading across a wide field dotted with red 1066 walk signs.

To Catsfield, via Steven's Crouch

5km

Go down the field, then up the steep hill ahead, crossing two little plank bridges over streams and passing through some woodland. At the top of the hill the path levels out and emerges into a large open field. Cross the faint track ahead through the field: you're heading for the left-hand side of the long line of woodland ahead. Pass a smaller patch of woodland on the left – further to the left is a Victorian Gothic stone cottage. Continue heading to the long patch of woodland, then go through the tip of it and up through the field – there's an enormous horse chestnut on the right, with heavy branches that touch the ground and look as if they're rerooting themselves. Follow the 1066 sign on a post on the left, which points you up the hill, towards the road. Just to the left is a stone gatehouse and a set of gateposts topped by statues of greyhounds.

A hundred metres beyond you join a road at the village of **Steven's Crouch** – you'll see some picturesque thatched, timber-framed cottages to the right. Cross a stile and turn left onto the road, then cross the road almost immediately and follow the sign that leads away from the road towards Catsfield. This leads down an avenue lined by tall Wellingtonia trees. After 350m you reach a junction; the road ahead has a "no entry" sign (this is the only point of the walk where the 1066 signs let you down). Go through the gate on the left, rather than turning down the no-entry road, then turn right down the track towards Catsfield, rather than curving up to the left. On the far side of the gate, the track leads downhill into pine woodland, passing a couple of lakes on the right after 800m. Some 800m further on, go through a gate, with a pond on the left, and join the road at **Catsfield**.

On to Battle

3.5km

Turn left and walk along the road for 400m through the undistinguished village. On the far side of the village you'll see a **1066 sign** on a telegraph pole. Turn left off the road at this sign, cross a field and then turn left briefly to reach a road. Cross the road and follow another 1066 sign which points off to the right along a track. Follow the track for 100m, continuing straight ahead over a stile and into a field. Go through a pine plantation – beyond the pines in the corner of field is a stile; follow the sign here which points left through the trees.

The path leads steeply downhill for 200m. Cross a stile onto a little gravel track. Ignore the turning signposted to Farthings and go straight ahead to Farthings Cottage. Follow the path past the cottage. Go through a metal gate and the path opens out into a field. Follow the sign which points ahead up a steep grassy hill and walk across and then down the field. At the end of the field the path joins gravel track – the houses at the top of the hill are in Battle, while the line of trees to your right conceals the site of the battle beyond. At the top of the track, immediately ahead of you, lies Battle Abbey.

Battle

Battle is a small and inoffensively touristy town, dominated by the gatehouse of the abbey around which it was built. The long main street is lined with mediocre eating places, the exception being *The Food Rooms*, a surprisingly hip and high-quality **deli-café** halfway up on the right-hand side. They also run the excellent if slightly pricey *Pilgrim's* restaurant (£15 for a set Sunday lunch), located in a magnificent thirteenth-century timbered building facing the abbey – there's a high, barn-like timber roof and a vast fireplace inside. You can sit outside in summer and admire the abbey gatehouse. The food is all prepared using fresh local ingredients.

The entrance fee to **Battle Abbey** allows you to explore the ruined monastery buildings and also to tour the battle site. The papal authorities insisted that William build the abbey as penance for the deaths resulting from the battle; building started in 1070, and the abbey was consecrated in 1094. You enter via the gatehouse, built in 1338 in an elegant synthesis of form and function – the high polygonal turrets are both formidable and beautiful. Of the complex of buildings beyond the gatehouse, the most intriguing and best preserved (with the exception of the Abbot's Hall, which is now a school and not open to the public) is the airy dormitory, its three chambers descending to accommodate the sloping ground and its long lines punctuated by slender lancet windows. You can also see the foundations of the abbey church, whose high altar is supposed to mark the spot where Harold fell.

Battle Abbey is open daily: April–Sept 10am–6pm; Oct 10am–5pm; Nov–March 10am–4pm; £4.50; EH.

The most intangible feature of the site – the **battle** itself – is nicely evoked by an audio tour (you get a free handset when you buy your ticket). In a non-partisan touch, the events of the day are recalled by both a fictional Saxon thane and a Norman knight, with the female perspective coming from Edith Swanneck, Harold's lover. You look out over the battle site from the high ground occupied by the shield wall of the Saxons, or can take an extended version of the tour and walk round the battle site. The Saxon army was famously exhausted by their victory over the Norwegians at the Battle of Stamford Bridge, and by the hasty march south to take on the Normans. The tactics of the Normans – as recalled by the outraged audio thane – included faked retreats by the mounted knights and the consequent slaughter of the pursuing Saxon foot soldiers. The Saxon line was broken and Harold was killed, though he's more likely to have been bludgeoned to death than killed by an arrow in his eye as shown in the Bayeux Tapestry.

Turning right out of the abbey gatehouse you soon come to the **Church of St Mary the Virgin**, which features a Romanesque nave, Norman font, rare fourteenth-century wall paintings and the gaudy gilded alabaster tomb of Sir Anthony Browns (to whom Henry VIII granted the abbey).

To reach the **train station**, follow the road beyond the church for 500m, then take the signed road down the hill to the left.

Chichester Harbour

Fishbourne to Bosham

Distance and difficulty: 9km; easy.
Trains: London Victoria/Waterloo to Fishbourne (change at Havant; every 30min; 1hr 40min); return from Fishbourne to London Waterloo (change at Havant; every 30min; 1hr 55min).
Map: OS Landranger 197: *Chichester and the South Downs*; OS Explorer 120: *Chichester*.

The short stretch of land covered by this walk is rich and distinctive, both in appearance and history. The walk leads from **Fishbourne**, site of **Fishbourne Palace**, one of the grandest Roman villas in Britain, across a sheltered peninsula to the Saxon settlement of **Bosham**. There are no open seascapes, but water is a constant presence, from the marshland south of Fishbourne, where dense clumps of reeds tower above you, to salty Bosham itself. Here the houses cling together as if to resist the tide that races up Bosham Channel – one of a series of inlets that comprise **Chichester Harbour** – and then recedes to leave a tangle of seaweed, shells, tiny crabs and other marine detritus.

To get to Bosham in time for lunch, you'll probably need to leave a visit to Fishbourne Palace to the end of the walk. Bear in mind also that the route can get extremely muddy, and come prepared.

Getting started

0.5km

From **Fishbourne station**, turn right, crossing the rail line, and straight ahead down the road in the direction of Fishbourne Palace (see below) – you'll see the palace signed off to the left, up Roman Way. To carry on to Bosham, go straight ahead, turning left at the end of the road onto the A259 towards Chichester. After 200m, cross to the *Bull's Head* pub. Just beyond the pub, take a right onto Mill Lane.

Fishbourne Palace

Fishbourne Palace was one of the very few Roman villas in Britain whose size and grandeur bore comparison to its continental counterparts. Originally a supply depot for the Roman army, the site was developed in the second half of the first century as the splendid palace of the Romanized Celtic aristocrat **Cogidubnus** (the villa may have been granted to him in reward for his loyalty to Rome during the onslaught of Boudicca). The villa was similar to those in Pompeii, featuring gardens and a courtyard surrounded by a colonnaded walk, and a vaulted audience chamber where the owner

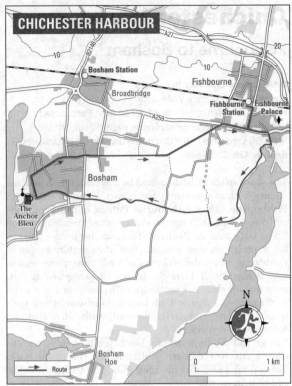

© Crown copyright

would receive guests. It also boasted baths and pools, and was adorned with mosaics, stuccowork, marble panels and elaborately painted frescoes, all thought to have been the work of highly skilled foreign craftsmen, though only the mosaic floors survive in anything but fragmentary form. The villa was destroyed by fire in the third century; charred door-sills are still visible between the mosaic floors. Bodies were buried in the ruins some time after the fire, and the skeleton of one still lies in situ in a shallow grave.

Fishbourne Palace is open Jan Sat & Sun 10am–4pm; Feb, Nov & Dec daily 10am–4pm; March–July, Sept & Oct daily 10am–5pm; Aug daily 10am–6pm; £5.

The palace's highlight is its series of fine **mosaic floors**, by far the most flamboyant and beautiful being the one which depicts Cupid riding a dolphin, surrounded by fantastic sea creatures. A jumble of artefacts is displayed in the palace **museum**, including roof tiles which acquired imprints of human and animal feet as they dried two thousand years ago, and a dainty intaglio onyx ring, engraved with a tiny image of a horse, a palm-frond waving above it. Otherwise, the palace is a bit of a disappointment. The surrounding houses and unattractive museum and shop have eradicated any atmosphere that may have clung to the site, and the style of interpretation throughout – particularly the shop-soiled dummies plonked in a crudely painted replica of a Roman room – is well past its sell-by date.

South along Chichester Channel

0.75km

Mill Lane leads to **Mill Pond**, opposite a beautiful thatched cottage. From the pond, public footpath signs point in three directions – take the right-hand path which goes past the pond and then winds through the high, rustling reeds, crossing a series of wooden bridges and trackways. This section is very watery at high tide – you may have to wait a little for it to recede. Eventually you come out onto a high bank on the edge of the mud flats which border the Chichester Channel, with a large, solitary oak in a field ahead of you. The landscape opens out and you can see boats either reposing on mud or bobbing in the water, depending on the state of the tide. You eventually descend from the bank and the path winds through a glade of low oak trees with a pond on the right – a good sheltered spot for a **picnic**.

Across the peninsula to Bosham

3km

Just beyond the glade, the path veers off to the right to cross the **peninsula** that separates the Chichester and Bosham channels. The path is wide and grassy at this point; where it reaches a T-junction after 300m, turn right and, 200m further on, turn left at the line of lime trees. After 500m, you cross a minor road; continue straight ahead, through wide, flat fields, broken up by patches of dense woodland. After passing a white cottage, the path widens to become a rough road. Where it curves round to the left, continue straight ahead, over a little wooden bridge. Almost immediately beyond here, a second bridge leads left, taking you straight towards a flint cottage.

Steps lead down to a minor road – cross this and carry on straight ahead between a house and a garage. The path leads through the back gardens of Bosham, and emerges at the harbour, where you get a sudden blast of salty air. Go straight along the edge of the harbour to the heart of Bosham.

Bosham

0.75km

The seventeenth- and eighteenth-century cottages of **Bosham** (pronounced "Bozzum") have a wonderfully organic quality, more redolent of a tumbling Cornish village than anything you'd expect to find in southeast England. The road round the harbour, **Mariner's Terrace**, takes you past terraced cottages and comes out at Beach Cottage (1708) – head straight up the road to reach the *Anchor Bleu* pub, and look out for the protective panels at the doorways of the houses you pass, which slot into stone grooves and protect against flooding at high tide.

The *Anchor Bleu* (☎01243/573956), licensed since the 1700s, is a characterful place with low beams, flagstones and a wheel-operated bulkhead door (for protection from high tides) leading to a little terrace with sea views. For lunch, it's best to go for the ploughman's rather than the cooked food, which can be pretty stodgy.

Turn left out of the pub to reach **Holy Trinity Church**, which sits on the lush Quay Meadow facing the water. The church is thought to be the oldest Christian site in Sussex, its unbuttressed, rocket-like tower unmistakably Saxon. Inside the church, the wide chancel arch gives the structure unexpected scale. The remains of an 8-year-old girl discovered in a tomb in the church in 1865 are thought to be those of **King Canute**'s daughter, who drowned in a mill stream behind the church. (It was also at Bosham that Canute famously ordered the sea to retreat. Contrary to popular belief, Canute knew he would fail, his purpose being to demonstrate both the limited powers he exercised as king, and his humility as a convert to Christianity.) The church's great antiquity is also reflected by its appearance in a panel of the **Bayeux Tapestry**, a replica of which hangs in the church, depicting King Harold leaving Bosham for Normandy in 1064, with the church in the background, so stylized as to be unrecognizable. It was an ill-starred trip, which ended in shipwreck and Harold being forced to swear an oath of allegiance to William, the future conqueror of England.

Back to Fishbourne

4km

If you're in a rush to get back to Fishbourne to see the palace before it closes, you could take the short but rather uninspiring circular return route from Bosham described below. However, if you're not in a hurry, the recommended **return route** is the way you came – the views of Chichester Cathedral, the intricate track through the marsh and the immense skies that seem magnified by the nearby water are well worth savouring twice.

To **return directly to Fishbourne** from the church, turn left past the *Anchor Bleu* back down to Beach Cottage. Turn left again and carry on straight ahead through the village. At the *Millstream Hotel*, follow the road round to the right. If you want to get to **Bosham station** (which, confusingly, is actually in the neighbouring village of **Broadbridge**) take the first left, 600m beyond the point where the road curves; the station is just over a kilometre up the road. Otherwise, just keep going up the road for another 500m.

Where the road curves round to the left, turn off the road and head along the path straight ahead, between the flint cottage and Rectory Farm – it's marked with a green public footpath sign. Ignore the public footpath sign to your left after 500m, and just keep going.

Where the path ends, continue ahead up the track, ignoring the public footpath sign to the left 200m beyond. There's a row of high lime trees to the right and the houses of Fishbourne are visible to the left. After another 600m, at the end of the track, go straight ahead. Turn right at the busy road and then left to reach the **station** and **Fishbourne Palace**, either on the signed footpath or on the road you came down earlier.

5

The North Wessex Downs to the New Forest

Much of the area covered by this chapter has a conspicuous sense of antiquity, dotted with stone monuments, burial mounds and hill forts which comprise the earliest evidence of the impact of Britons on their natural environment. Nowhere is this more apparent than at **Stonehenge**, the most famous prehistoric structure in Europe, which sits in the middle of the downs of Salisbury Plain while, just to the north, the **North Wessex Downs** – a vast tract of chalky downland and ancient woodland, stretching from the edge of the Chilterns in the east to the Vale of the White Horse in the west – are home to a rich assortment of ancient monuments. To the southeast of Salisbury is the **New Forest**, a swathe of forest, heath and bog which has a striking wilderness feel, belying the fact that it has been systematically managed since the Norman period.

The first walk in this chapter is along part of the **Ridgeway**, thought to be the oldest surviving road in Britain, taking you across the North Wessex Downs from just outside Swindon, via the Vale of the White Horse, to the pretty Oxfordshire village of Goring. It's designed as a two-day walk with an overnight stop at the first-rate *Ridgeway Youth Hostel*, but if you want to do just one day, make it the first, which includes a glut of extraordinary prehistoric monuments. The **North Wessex Downs** walk takes you to the highest point of the downs, Inkpen Hill, which is surmounted by a Neolithic burial mound, an Iron Age hillfort and a weird gibbet dating back to the seventeenth century. The third walk leads from Salisbury, via the remains of Old Sarum, up a lush river valley to **Stonehenge**, giving unforgettable long-range views of the imposing, ineffably mysterious monument. The final route in the chapter is a shortish **New Forest** walk, designed to take in the variety of landscapes that this wonderfully distinctive region offers, as well as a thousand-year old pub.

Thanks to efficient (though pricey) **train services**, these places can be reached in just over an hour. The exception is the New Forest, which takes 1hr 40min to get to – the walk is relatively short, to take account of the length of the journey. Whizzy trains for Swindon depart from **Paddington**. Trains for Kintbury, for the North Wessex Downs walk, also leave from Paddington, with additional stops at Ealing Broadway and Slough. Services for Salisbury leave from **Waterloo** and call at Clapham Junction. For the New Forest walk, trains leave from Waterloo, and also stop at Clapham Junction. If you fancy a **late start**, the North Wessex Downs walk is a good option – you don't have to start walking till noon. This and the Stonehenge walks are the easiest options for **drivers**.

The Ridgeway

Foxhill to Wantage and Goring

Distance and difficulty: day 1: 17.5km; day 2: 25km; strenuous.
Trains: London Paddington to Swindon (every 20min; 1hr); return from Goring to London Paddington (every 15min; 1hr).
Map: OS Landranger map 174: *Newbury & Wantage*; OS Explorer 170: *Abingdon, Wantage & Vale of White Horse.*

The **Ridgeway**, a 136-kilometre path starting at Overton Hill in Wiltshire and ending at Ivinghoe Beacon in Buckinghamshire, formed part of an ancient **trading route** between southwest England and mainland Europe, which may have started on the Dorset coast and run up to Norfolk. The route has been used by traders, invaders and drovers for at least five thousand years, the proliferation of Neolithic and Bronze Age burial sites and Iron Age forts along the way attesting to its cultural and strategic importance. The Ridgeway was the scene of skirmishes between the Saxons, under Alfred the Great (see box on p.124), and the Vikings, who sought to use it to penetrate the kingdom of Wessex. Its primary purpose in the medieval period was as a drove road between Wales and the home counties. Until the Enclosure Acts of 1750 there probably never was one specific road – the modern Ridgeway is an amalgam of several smaller routes, and originally people would have used the easiest and driest section available on the day.

The section of the Ridgeway covered here leads east from **Foxhill** to the **Vale of the White Horse**, passing some of England's most intriguing prehistoric sites including Wayland's Smithy, Uffington Castle and the White Horse itself. You can return to London via **Wantage** at the end of day one, or stay at the spectacular youth hostel just off the route and continue for a second day to the village of **Goring**, sitting in a gentle bend of the River Thames. If you only do one day of this walk, make sure it's the first; the landscape is pleasant on day two, but there are no dramatic sights.

The modern route is clearly **marked** for most of its way, and though many other public footpaths cross it, the Ridgeway continues on its inexorable run from west to east. If in doubt, aim for the high ground.

Day one

17.5km

The first day of the walk is crammed with interest, from medieval field terraces to the cluster of superb prehistoric sights at the **Vale of the White Horse**. The pubs to the north of the Ridgeway at Ashbury, Woolstone and Kingston

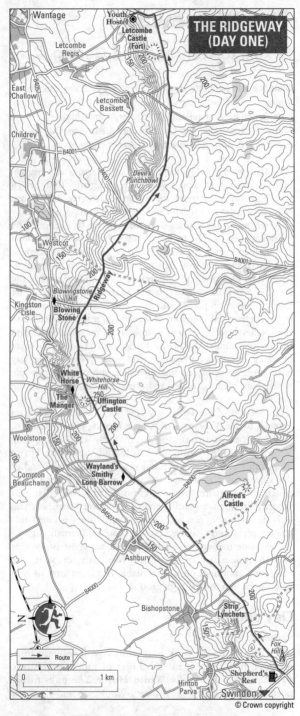

Lisle all make decent **lunch** stops, although as these all involve a 3km detour from the Ridgeway, you might prefer to take a picnic lunch. Day one ends near **Wantage** – you can either get a taxi into town for the station if you want to end your walk, or stay at the **Ridgeway Youth Hostel**, which lies just off the route.

Getting started

Walk straight ahead out of **Swindon station** and up Wellington Street to the **bus station**, and take bus #46, #48 or #48a to Foxhill (Mon–Fri hourly, Sat every 40min; 25min; ☎01793/428428); ask the driver to drop you at the *Shepherd's Rest* pub. A **taxi** (☎01793/766666) to Foxhill will cost around £10.

Foxhill and the Strip Lynchets

5km

Get off the bus at **Foxhill** (there's a row of terraced cottages on the right) and, with the *Shepherd's Rest* on your left, head straight up the sealed minor road following the sign to the village of Hinton Parva. After 200m, follow a second sign, on the right, which signals the start of this stage of the **Ridgeway**. Head along the Ridgeway, ignoring the public path which leads off to Charlbury Hill after around 750m, beyond which the path ascends quite steeply for 500m, over the brow of the hill, with the tumulus of **Lammy Down** visible to the right.

A worthwhile **detour** leads left for 200m down a path (marked with a Countryside Commission sign) to the **Strip Lynchets**, a well-preserved example of the medieval system of field terracing. These grassy steps sit in a lovely valley, with glorious views ahead to the green swell of Uffington Castle and down to the village of Bishopstone.

Returning to the Ridgeway, you descend steadily for another three kilometres, crossing two minor roads, the first to Bishopstone and the second to Idstone. Just beyond the Idstone turn-off, down to the right, is the small Iron Age fort of **Alfred's Castle**, where Alfred fought the Danes in 871. This piece of ground was earlier developed by the Romans, and traces of what may have been a villa or temple have been excavated, along with a cache of ten babies' skeletons. Roman law did not permit burial within towns or forts, but babies under ten days old were exempt from this, as they were not classed as citizens.

Wayland's Smithy

1.5km

Returning to the Ridgeway, it's another 1.5km to the atmospheric Neolithic tomb of **Wayland's Smithy**; cross the road to Ashdown and walk through a strip of woodland, and the

Alfred the Great

. . . he seems to me a very foolish man, and very wretched, who will not increase his understanding while he is in the world, and ever wish and long to reach that endless life where all shall be made clear.

Alfred the Great

The first written mention of the Ridgeway is in the **Anglo Saxon Chronicle**, which describes Danish raiders sweeping along the route, from Ashdown to Scutchamer Knob. The chronicle was in part a record of the exploits of the scholar-king **Alfred the Great**, who almost certainly commissioned it. Alfred's military achievements are recalled in sites along the route of the Ridgeway, from the battle ground at Ashdown (see p.123) to the Blowing Stone (see p.126). Lying low during a lull between battles, this local lad, born in Wantage in 849, famously allowed himself to be scolded by a peasant woman for leaving her cakes to burn. He was venerated, in his time and even now, more than a thousand years later, both as a brilliant general and as a protector of the poor.

Alfred began his onslaught against the Danes during the reign of his brother Ethelred, culminating in the famous victory at the **Battle of Ashdown** in 871. The following year Ethelred died, and Alfred became king of Wessex. Periods of peace alternated with renewed Danish attacks, until Alfred finally defeated the invaders once and for all in 897. One of his innovations as a tactician was the establishment of fortified burghs – grass-covered earthworks which are still a part of the landscape of the Ridgeway.

A thoughtful and inspired peacetime leader, Alfred used the lulls between conflicts to focus on civic reorganization. The monasteries, shattered by the Danes, were re-established as centres of learning, and Alfred founded schools in Oxford, even learning Latin himself in middle age and making translations of books of theology, history and philosophy, which he freely infused with his own thoughts, thus contributing to the earliest English literature.

tomb's tall sarsen stones can just be seen to the left in a stately circle of beech trees.

Wayland's Smithy is thought to be 5500 years old, and originally comprised a wooden, tent-shaped chamber containing the remains of fourteen people. Around 3300 BC, a longer cruciform tomb was built on top of the old one, which was covered over with a mound of chalk and stone. The three stone chambers of the more recent tomb were excavated in the 1920s, and eight bodies were found. The tomb acquired its name when the Saxons stumbled upon it and, ignorant of its real function, appropriated it for their god, Wayland the Smith; it was said that Wayland would shoe travellers' horses if they left a penny on the capstone of the tomb. You may see various offerings of flowers, grain, fruit and feathers around the tomb, left by New Age types.

The Vale of the White Horse

1.5km

Some 1.5km beyond Wayland's Smithy, the Ridgeway climbs a steepish hill to reach the **Vale of the White Horse**, a unique collection of prehistoric sights; cross the stile on the left where you'll see a National Trust sign, and continue up to the brow of the hill.

The landscape opens out to reveal the great circular earthwork of **Uffington Castle**, built between 300 BC and 43 AD and encircled by a bank and ditch, now eroded and grazed by sheep and scattered with field scabious, poppies, pyramidal orchids and cowslips. The "castle" – or, more accurately, fort – is roughly oval in shape and eight acres in extent. It had a single entrance to the northwest and its ramparts would have been faced with sarsen stone. One in a chain of such defensive structures, it's thought that Uffington Castle was built to protect travellers along the Ridgeway from attack from the north.

About 200m beyond the fort, the land tumbles vertiginously down to the undulating glacial valley called the **Manger**. Obscured by the steepness of the valley wall until you are almost upon it is the **White Horse** (the legend is that the horse comes down off its hill at night to graze in the Manger). It was popularly thought that the 114-metre-long horse was cut into the turf to commemorate Alfred's victory over the Danes, but in fact it's much more ancient, being the oldest chalk figure in the country and dating back three thousand years. One of the many curious things about the horse is that its shape can only properly be seen from a distance because of the curve of the hill – the best view is from one of the little biplanes that buzz overhead. Nearby signs feature a drawing of the horse, which will help you appreciate the figure's abstract beauty: it looks as if it was sketched by Picasso in a few deft strokes. The local legend which asserts that "while men sleep the horse climbs up the hill" is not as whimsical as it sounds; the upper edges of the chalk lines are gradually eroding and the lower edges silting up, causing the horse to edge up the hillside. Fairs at Uffington Castle, the first record of which is in 1677, were held every seven years or so until 1857; 30,000 people were said to have attended in 1780. These were celebratory occasions when the White Horse was "scoured", or cleaned; the maintenance of the horse was one of the conditions by which the lord of the manor held his land. Horse and ass races were a feature of the fair, as was the bizarre practice of sliding down the hill on a horse's jawbone, according to one eighteenth-century account.

Just below the horse is a small artificial hillock, **Dragon's Hill**, which, according to local legend, is where St George killed the dragon. Two oval mounds between the horse and the fort were excavated in 1857 and found to contain fifty Roman skeletons. Five of the bodies held coins between their teeth, to pay the ferryman to carry them over the River Styx into the underworld.

The White Horse to the Blowing Stone

2.5km

Continue for 2.5km to the next minor road which crosses the Ridgeway – to the left down the hill is to the village of Kingstone Lisle. On the right, towards the bottom of the hill, you can detour off the Ridgeway for 1.5km to the garden of a neat cottage which encloses the **Blowing Stone**, a rough block of sarsen which resembles a holey cheese (though it's quite a steep hill, so only make the detour if you're feeling energetic). The legend connected with the stone is that King Alfred blew into it to call the Saxons to fight the Danes. With some determination you can produce a strange booming sound by blowing into one of the holes in the stone; local advice is to blow a raspberry into it, covering the hole completely with your mouth – and try not to think of all the congealed spit which covers the hole.

....

If you fancy a pub stop at this point, cross the B4507, which cuts across Blowingstone Hill, and carry straight on for 700m past the idyllic thatched cottages and country gardens of Kingston Lisle, bearing right at the junction for the *Blowingstone Inn* (℡01367/820288), a gentrified but pleasant pub.

....

To Segsbury Castle and the youth hostel

7km

Back on the Ridgeway, past long lines of gallops – fenced areas used for exercising race horses – the route ascends **Sparsholt Down**; you'll see a radio mast on the right-hand side and a farm and paddock where there's a **drinking-water tap**. Turn right onto the sealed road which crosses the **B4001** to Wantage; the Ridgeway resumes opposite the give way sign.

The grassy ground to the left of the Ridgeway falls dramatically away to form a smooth valley called the **Devil's Punchbowl**. After 1.5km, you cross a track which runs north to **Letcombe Bassett**, immortalized as Cresscombe in Hardy's *Jude the Obscure*.

Around 1.5km from here, a broad track to the right opposite some corrugated-iron farm buildings leads for 100m to another Iron Age relic, **Segsbury Castle**. It was, according to an eighteenth-century account, fronted by tall sarsen stones – these have since been removed and all you see now is a steep grassy mound. Nineteenth-century excavations uncovered human bones in a stone chamber, flint scrapers and pottery, plus what is thought to be a boss from a Saxon shield.

If you're doing both days of the walk, you can spend the night at the excellent **Ridgeway Youth Hostel** (℡01235/760253; Ⓦwww.yharidgeway.org.uk; £11.50 per person): turn left onto the **A338**, past Redhouse Cottage, and go down the hill. It's a very attractive building, comprising several disused barns and designed to exploit the superb views of the valley below. The dorms resemble wooden ship berths, and there's a sense of space and light throughout. Aim to arrive by 6pm, so you can order dinner for around a fiver, or order it by phone in advance. Breakfast is also available and there's a shop selling drinks and chocolate as well as packed lunches, which can be ordered up to 10.30pm the night before – a good option if you don't want to detour away from the Ridgeway on day two.

If you want to end your walk here, a taxi
(call ℡01235/762035) from the youth hostel to Wantage
will cost around £5.

Day two

25km

The second day of the walk is less exciting than the first, although the Saxon burial mound at **Scutchamer Knob** provides some atmosphere, and there's a good pub **lunch** detour to East Ilsley. The walk ends at the pretty conjoined villages of **Streatley** and **Goring**.

Towards Scutchamer Knob

7km

To return to the Ridgeway, turn right out of the youth hostel and back up the A338, then take the signed turning to the left. The route, paved for the first 400m, leads past farm buildings and paddocks, passing a wood. After just over 1km the route divides into two wide paths – follow the one to the left. Cross the B4494 to Wantage, beyond which you'll come to a needle-like **monument** to the right of the route, erected by Baroness Wantage in 1901 in memory of her husband, the Baron of Wantage.

Scutchamer Knob towards Rodden Downs

6.5km

Three kilometres past the monument is the easy-to-miss **Scutchamer Knob** (it lies in a little copse off to the right,

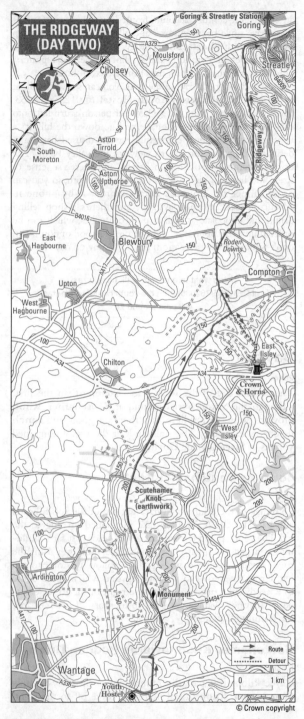

THE RIDGEWAY (DAY TWO)

opposite a "Respect the Ridgeway" sign). A horseshoe-shaped mound of earth, Scutchamer Knob is thought to be the burial place of the Saxon king **Cwicchelm**, who died in 593 AD. Whatever the mound's original function, it's a restful spot, with views over the rolling fields to the south. Just south of here, off the Ridgeway, is one of several "**Starveall Farms**", the name perhaps an echo of an ancient famine. Other settlements along the route – Woolpack and Woolstone, for example – recall the area's wealth in wool and meat during the Middle Ages, when the Ridgeway was used as a drove road.

Cross the minor road to East Hendred. On the far side, you'll see lines of gallops in the field to the right – many racehorses are trained and stabled around here. The panorama also takes in one of the few signs of industrial England visible on the walk, **Didcot Power Station**, almost ten kilometres away. When permission was given to build the power station, it was on condition that it was modified, with six cooling towers grouped in two groups of three rather than the usual eight grouped in two groups of four, supposedly to make it more attractive.

After 500m you cross another minor road, walking through a small car park; 1.5km from here the route dips under the busy **A34**. Soon after this, on the right, you'll find a handy **drinking-water tap**.

Over Rodden Downs

5km

For a short stretch beyond the underpass the Ridgeway is paved; 2.5km beyond the underpass you reach a crossroads: bear left to stay on the Ridgeway. If you fancy a diversion for a **pub lunch**, take a right to the village of **East Ilsley**, 1.5km distant. Sheep fairs were held at East Ilsley for hundreds of years – in the mid-eighteenth century around 80,000 sheep were sold at its annual fair, and there were thirteen pubs to sustain the drovers and farmers.

....

The welcoming *Crown and Horns* (☎01635/281545) in East Ilsley serves sturdy pub food and real ales – there's outdoor seating in the stable yard.

....

Continuing along the Ridgeway, the route ascends **Rodden Downs**. Go straight ahead at the crossroads 2.5km beyond the East Ilsley turn-off; the left-hand fork runs up to **Lowbury Hill** which is said to be haunted, perhaps by the Roman woman who was found buried here under an earth bank.

To Streatley and Goring

6.5km

The landscape opens out for the gradual descent towards

Streatley, with undulating fields to either side. The path drops through a wooded avenue to a thatched cottage and farm, then bears left. From this point the remainder of the walk is on a sealed road. You pass a row of red-brick terraced houses to the right; ignore the two public footpath signs leading off to the right.

Continue along the road and, at the give way sign, turn right onto the A417 to Streatley and bear right again at the second give way sign. Carry on for another 300m and you'll come to the handsome *Bull* **pub**, which may be a very welcome sight at this stage. Opposite the pub, the turning to the left leads down, past an attractive jumble of brick, flint and thatched houses, towards the Thames. Just before you cross the river, you could detour 50m to the left to **St Mary's**, a pretty thirteenth-century church that was heavily restored – though in an uncharacteristically plain way – by the Victorians.

A double-humped bridge takes you across the river to **Goring**. Off to the right is the handsome Norman church of **St Thomas**. The interior is in an attractive state of faint decay, with peeling paint and metal braces straining round huge circular columns. To reach **Goring station**, head straight up the hill and turn right after the railway bridge.

The North Wessex Downs

Kintbury to Inkpen and back

Distance and difficulty: 16km; moderate to strenuous.
Train: London Paddington to Kintbury (hourly; 1hr 15min); return
from Kintbury to London Paddington (hourly; 1hr 15min).
Map: OS Landranger 174: *Newbury & Wantage*; OS Explorer
158: *Newbury & Hungerford*.

The **North Wessex Downs** reach their highest point at
Inkpen Hill, between Newbury and Hungerford, which is
crowned by the remains of a vast Iron Age fort and a long
barrow, still surmounted by a gibbet that was originally erected in the seventeenth century. The walk starts from the village of **Kintbury**, sitting snug in the valley of the Kennet,
and goes across farmland to **Inkpen**, a ramblingly attractive
village where the friendly *Swan* serves up fine organic pub
lunches. From Inkpen it's a steep but short scramble up onto the ridge of the downs, where the sweeping long views
take in five counties. Paths and minor roads bring you in a
circle back to Kintbury, where the *Dundas Arms*, sitting prettily on the river, is a great spot to wait for your train home.

Kintbury to The Swan
5km

From the station, head left towards the *Dundas Arms*. Cross
the canal at Kintbury Lock, and then the river, where you'll
see a weir up to the right. Go straight up the road, which
curves to the right through the village. Just past the *Blue Ball*
pub on the right, follow Wallington's Road to the left, a dead
end which leads towards the St Cassian Centre, a Catholic
youth retreat.

After 500m, take the signposted public footpath to the left,
rather than the private road to St Cassians. After 200m you'll
reach some dilapidated farm buildings. Follow the public footpath sign which points across the fields to the right, then cross
the road 150m beyond and carry on up the field, with St
Cassian's to the left. Go through a patch of woodland for 250m
to emerge into a field; head diagonally across the field, onto a
minor road and turn right. Head down the drive which leads
past **Balsdon Farm** (don't be deterred by the "private" signs –
this isn't a bridleway, but it is a public footpath).

You emerge beyond the farm at some signposts; follow the
public footpath sign to the left, rather than the bridleway
sign. Ahead you can see the ridge of the downs. After 100m,
cross the plank bridge over a stream – another 600m further

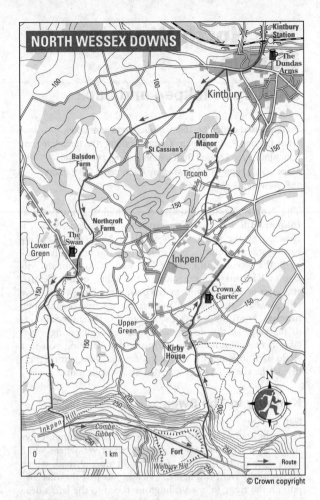

© Crown copyright

on, you'll see the prettily dilapidated buildings of Northcroft Farm to the left. Where the path comes out on a minor road, turn right and follow the road for 500m until you get to a small, triangular green and a red phone box. This is the western edge of Inkpen, known as **Lower Green**.

Turn right past the grandiose mock-Georgian houses, untypical of this otherwise modest village, and right again to reach the seventeenth-century **Swan** pub.

> *The Swan* (☎ 01488/668326) has been rather over-gentrified, but there's nice terraced seating outside and the food is excellent, with local organic meat – try the sausages – plus plenty of veggie options and home-made puddings, which come with large dollops of organic clotted cream. There's an organic farm shop attached to the pub.

Inkpen Hill

5km

From the pub, go back up the road to the phone box and then straight ahead along the road signed towards Combe and Ham. The road curves round to the right; after 250m you'll see thirteenth-century **Inkpen Church** a couple of hundred metres away to the left – continue following the road as it curves round to the right. Some 200m past the church, follow the public footpath sign pointing to the left and go along this track which leads up to the long grassy ridge of the **downs** – the gibbet (see below) is visible on top of the hill ahead of you. Go through an avenue of trees for 400m, after which the path begins to climb the steep hill. After 100m, it's joined by a grassy track leading diagonally to the left up the hill. Don't turn left on the first path you reach at the top of the ridge (which leads down the ridge and away from the fort); instead, keep going for 50m or so until you reach a track enclosed by fences. Turn left here, towards the gibbet.

Combe Gibbet long barrow, 600m further on, dates from around 3500 BC, which makes it even older than the similar Wayland's Smithy on the nearby Ridgeway (see p.123). Little is known about the site, which has never been excavated, but as well as being a burial mound, its prominent position suggests it delineated the territory of the people who built it. The **gibbet** was first erected in 1676 to hang creepy locals George Broomham and his mistress Dorothy Newman – the pair murdered George's wife and son, but were seen by the village idiot, "Mad Thomas". They were hanged from either side of the gibbet, which explains its unusual shape – most gibbets have just one arm. This is not the original gibbet: the structure has been replaced several times over the centuries. The first gibbet rotted away, the second was struck by lightning, and the third was blown over in a storm in 1949. The people of Inkpen, however, had by this time become so fond of the cheerful sight of a gibbet looming over their village that they clubbed together for a new one, which was made of oak and erected in 1950.

Carry on along the chalky track past the gibbet and the car park onto **Walbury Hill** – take the middle track beyond the car park to ascend the bank of the early Iron Age hillfort. Walk straight ahead, across the fort – the largest in the country, it stretches for 700m.

Back to Kintbury

6km

A hundred metres beyond the fort, between it and the next car park, follow the signed public footpath to the left, which leads down across the hill (ahead in the distance, you can see Kirby House, which you'll pass later). Descend the hill to a wire fence and climb through it onto a **minor road** – you'll see a public footpath sign on the other side of the road. Turn left onto the road and continue 500m to a junction, then go straight ahead, following the signs to Inkpen. A kilometre beyond lies **Kirby House**, an elegantly proportioned Queen Anne country mansion, flanked by avenues of trees and stable buildings.

Just past Kirby House, follow the sign on the right along the road to Kintbury. After 500m you come out at a junction; immediately to the right is the *Crown & Garter* – turn right and go past the pub, and then, after another 200m, past a row of white houses on the left and a silver-birch wood to the right. A hundred metres beyond the houses, take the public bridleway to the left, signed to "PO and Folly roads". This track passes a couple of farms, and then after 250m dips down into woodland and over a little bridge. Head up the hill out of the woods and onto a narrow track. Ignore the public bridleway sign to the left and go straight ahead, following the public footpath sign through what looks like a private garden, with a small gazebo to your right. At the end of the lawn you'll see a public footpath sign; follow this past a handful of houses on the outer edge of Inkpen.

Cross the road here, after which you soon leave the houses behind, heading downhill through a field. Go through the squeeze gate and down through another field. At the end of the field you emerge at a post with public footpath signs, which point back the way you came and to the left; go straight ahead here, down the road, ignoring the public footpath sign 200m further on to the right. Ahead, you can make out **Titcomb Manor**, but before you reach it go through the squeeze gate on the right and turn left. Halfway across the field, you come to a public footpath sign pointing right – follow it across the field to the wooden gate marked with public right of way signs. Cross the stile over the fence and turn left, going along the edge of the field. Cross the bridge and almost immediately turn left over another stile, then go through a tunnel of trees to emerge onto the High Street in Kintbury, opposite the *Blue Ball*. Turn right to get back to the **station**.

The Normanton Down Barrows

3km

The path emerges at a minor road; cross this and go through the gate ahead of you, where you'll see public footpath signs (the distinct mound of a tumulus can be seen just off the path and down to the right). Carry on straight ahead up the field, keeping its boundary and the wood to your immediate left; down the hill to the right you'll see Lake House, a graceful Jacobean manor that's home to Sting and his wife Trudi Styler, who penned the *Lake House Cookbook* with the assistance of their "family chef".

Continue down the path to reach a stile to the right of a metal gate – cross this and head down the path. Go straight down the field towards the white sign, then turn left on the chalky road, following the byway sign. The track then divides – the track to the left is private, so carry on straight ahead past the paddocks. At **Springbottom Farm**, turn left past the big barn. The track then splits – take the right-hand fork.

There's a long ascent of the hill ahead, up the wide grassy path; if you're beginning to flag, you'll be revived by the extraordinary first sight from the top of **Stonehenge**, the focal point of endless downland. One of the strange properties of the stones is the way their proportions appear to change: from this distance they appear elongated and hugely tall, like a megalithic Manhattan; a little nearer and they seem rather squat; while when you're up as close as you're permitted to get they are broodingly large.

The ridge commanding this spectacular view is capped by the **Normanton Down Barrows**, a line of low mounds to your left and right. They lie on private farmland and aren't accessible to the public. The barrows stretch for 750m, and include the early Bronze Age **Bush Barrow**, where the most significant finds were uncovered – the barrow contained the grave of a tall, stout man who was buried with artefacts to carry to the afterlife, including a bronze axe, a spearhead and a dagger.

Stonehenge

1.5km

Stonehenge is pinned between the thunderingly busy A303 and the A344; it's a tribute to the special qualities of the place that any atmosphere survives the roar of traffic and attendant touristy tat – one advantage of the first distant view of Stonehenge is that the A303 is for the moment tucked into a fold of the downs, though as you continue it becomes all too evident. Plans to bury the roads have been in the offing for years, but arguments continue over what type of tunnelling to use.

Just beyond the Normanton Down Barrows, turn left through a field for 300m, then turn right at the National

Stonehenge and the druids

Modern fascination with the **druids**, fuelled by lurid tales of sacrifice and magic rites, can be dated to the Renaissance and the rebirth of interest in the Classical world. Descriptions of the druids come from Classical writers such as Pliny, Tacitus and Julius Caesar – Caesar wrote that the druids "know much about the stars and celestial motions, and about the size of the earth and the universe, and about the essential nature of things, and about the powers and authority of the immortal gods; and these things they teach to their pupils".

There are no physical descriptions of druids, but it is probably because of the connection with Roman writers that, in the popular imagination, they come clad in white, toga-like garments. All that's known for certain about the druids is that they formed a class of priests, practised a religion dictated by nature and the seasons, and that they performed animal and human sacrifices.

Seventeenth- and eighteenth-century antiquarians such as **John Aubrey** and **William Stukeley** seized on these Classical descriptions – it was they who made the speculative connection between the druids and the building of Stonehenge, even though Classical descriptions of druidic rites place them firmly in the natural world, amongst groves and springs, suggesting that they would have had little interest in fashioning the enormous megaliths of Stonehenge.

Subsequent events further obfuscated the real identity of the druids. William Stukeley is thought to have founded the **First Order of Druids** in Primrose Hill in London in 1717, a quasi-mystical order that also took inspiration from freemasonry. This was supplanted by the **Ancient Order of Druids**, which continued through the nineteenth century and into the twentieth – Winston Churchill was a member, hosting a gathering of "druids" at Blenheim Palace in 1908.

Exactly when the first **summer solstice** celebrations were held at Stonehenge is unclear, but by 1900 the then owner of Stonehenge, Sir Edward Antrobus, was so alarmed by the numbers attending the rites that he had the site fenced in and imposed an entry fee – the druids were outraged and refused to pay. The annual celebrations continued, though, and eventually took on a less ritualistic and more celebratory character; by the 1970s, the masonic form of druidism had been replaced by hippy-influenced neo-paganism. Clashes between the police and summer-solstice worshippers became an annual occurrence, reaching a climax at the "Battle of the Beanfield" in 1985, when 700 people were arrested. The six-kilometre exclusion zone that used to operate was abandoned in 1999, and access is now permitted on the solstice.

To Pilley

1.5km

At the end of the reserve you reach a gate – go through and continue straight ahead for 300m to reach a road, then turn right up the hill towards Pilley. After 200m you'll see a sign on the right pointing to **Spinner's Garden** (mid-April to mid-Sept 10am–5pm; £2; mid-Sept to mid-April; free, though the garden is only partly open); it's worth a visit if you have an interest in gardening and is only another 200m off the road. Built on a slope overlooking the river valley, this luxuriant and exotic woodland garden is planted with azaleas, rhododendrons and magnolias, interspersed with curly ferns, irises and rare shrubs such as the purple Judas Tree.

The thatched *Fleur de Lys* **pub**, 300m beyond the turn-off to the garden, on the straggling outskirts of **Pilley**, is a proto-

The laws of the New Forest

The **New Forest** was named by William the Conqueror in 1079, when he established it as his personal hunting ground. He and his son, William Rufus, ruled over it with an iron hand, imposing violent penalties on poachers, from mutilation to execution. The locals must have breathed a sigh of relief when nasty Rufus, named for his rosy features, was killed in the forest in 1100 in a "hunting accident" (most probably a political assassination).

The **Charter of the Forest**, drawn up in 1217, modified forest law in favour of the inhabitants, who are still known as **Commoners**. Commoners' rights, framed in arcane medieval language, include "turbary" (the right to cut peat or turf as fuel); "estovers" (the right to collect firewood); and "mast" (the right to turn pigs out during a period known as "pannage"). This system is maintained by the **Verderers Court**, one of the oldest judicial courts in Britain. The Verderers were originally charged with implementing the harsh Norman laws, but in 1877 the largely defunct court was reinvented, and it now upholds the rights of Commoners and oversees the health and welfare of the forest animals. The Verderers meet ten times a year in the seventeenth-century **Verderer's Hall** in Lyndhurst, where the Crown Stirrup is also preserved – in Norman times, any dog too large to fit through the stirrup was lamed so that it couldn't chase deer. The eleven Verderers appoint six **Agisters**, who manage the five thousand ponies and cattle that roam the forest.

Much of the forest is still crown land, managed for recreation and timber production. This continues a long forest tradition: records dating from 1611 testify to the forest's importance in providing oak for warships, each of which required the felling of at least sixty trees. Despite such logging, there has always been an emphasis on the good environmental management of this land – indeed the desire to safeguard the forest led to the implementation, in 1483, of the first ever parliamentary act on tree protection.

typical English pub of great antiquity: they claim to have been serving up drinks since 1096, and you'll see a list of landlords going back to 1498 on the way in.

....

The bar menu at the *Fleur de Lys* (℡01590/672158) has a "carnivore" section, with meaty options including game pie and local sausages, but there's plenty of choice for veggies as well. There are good guest ales on tap, and a pretty garden at the back.

....

Coming out of the pub, turn right and head up the road through the village. You pass the Working Men's Club on your right and the "Pilley" sign, and cross a cattlegrid. Walk for 300m along the main road until it bends sharp right, where you take the little paved path to the left – May Lane. After 100m you reach a "no parking" sign on the left and after a further 50m there's a footpath sign on the right. Follow this across the field, along the slightly ridged grassy path, to reach a line of trees on the far side of the field, then turn left immediately you pass the trees (unless you want to make a detour onto Beaulieu Heath, in which case turn right).

Beaulieu Heath is a great open expanse, its fourteen-kilometre circumference framed by woodland. The heath's thin soil supports a meagre covering of heather and gorse, but the boggy areas are rich in rare plant and insect life. Even on a short detour onto the heath you can get a real sense of isolation, but bear in mind that the paths across it are unmarked and faint, and can easily be confused with tracks made by the pint-sized ponies. The lack of clearly definable tracks makes it impossible to describe a route here – if you do want to venture out onto the heath, arm yourself with OS Explorer 22: *New Forest*.

To Roydon Wood

6km

You'll see two footpaths ahead – a bridleway on the left and a footpath over a stile to the right. Take the latter and go diagonally through the woods until, after 50m, you emerge at the bottom right-hand side of a clearing. Head towards the top left-hand side of the clearing, from where a path leads through the trees and then straight ahead across the fields for 700m. You come out onto crossroads – go down the paved road to the right for 200m to the Norman and medieval **Church of St John the Baptist**. Unusually, the church, which sits on a mound, is in an isolated position away from any village – it's thought to have been built on the site of a prehistoric place of worship. The writer and illustrator **William Gilpin** was rector here in the late eighteenth century and wrote scathingly about the "indolent race" of foresters who marred the serenity of the New Forest by "forest pilfer . . . deer stealing, poaching or purloining timber".

From the church, follow the footpath sign towards the car park, where you'll see a yellow arrow on the fence post ahead of you, pointing forwards. This path emerges after 200m at **Haywards Farm**; turn left onto the gravel road and continue ahead, ignoring the private road which goes off to the right after 700m and carrying on for another 600m. Approaching Dilton Farm, which you'll see ahead of you, take the track that curves round to the left, marked with a blue bridleway sign, rather than going straight ahead to the farm.

You're now in **Roydon Wood Nature Reserve**, an area of broad-leaf woodland, some of it ancient and undisturbed. Just over a kilometre into the wood you come to a junction, with bridleway signs pointing to the left and right – turn left and head down the hill to cross the wooden bridge over the Lymington River. Up to the right is **Roydon Manor**, a modest seventeenth-century brick mansion, thought to have to have been a chapel of the Knights Templar.

The path comes out onto a track. Turn right here following the bridleway sign, which leads after 200m to a red-brick cottage. Turn left up the hill for 100m then follow the wiggly bridleway ahead of you, rather than continuing along the track, which curves to the left. The track continues through the woods for 700m, dipping down and then climbing steeply before coming out of the trees along the field edge to the right into Brockenhurst Park and then joining a minor road.

Brockenhurst

1km

Turn right along the road and walk 200m to reach the **Church of St Nicholas**, the oldest church in the New Forest – Christians have worshipped on this site since the eighth century. Some Saxon herring-bone stonework survives in the south wall of the nave, though the building is mainly Norman, with an eighteenth-century brick tower and Victorian additions. The dark shaggy yew tree next to the church is at least a thousand years old. In the graveyard are buried a hundred casualties of World War I, among them 93 New Zealanders, one Australian and three Indians, brought from French battlefields to be treated at Brockenhurst Hospital. Don't miss the curious grave of local snake-catcher **"Brusher" Mills**, depicting a bearded Brusher with the tools of his trade – a forked stick and sack. Brusher lived in a hut in the forest and took up snake-catching in the 1880s; some of his snakes were sent to London Zoo to feed the birds of prey, while others were used to make ointments. Brusher once emptied a bag of snakes onto the floor of his regular, the *Railway Inn* in Brockenhurst (now called the *Snake Catcher*), to help clear a path to the bar.

Beyond the church, carry on down the road for 300m to a busy road – cross it to reach **Brockenhurst station**.

6

The Thames Valley

Perhaps the most marked characteristic of the **Thames Valley** is – as it has been for centuries – affluence. The stretch of the river immediately to the west of London has long provided an escape from the capital for those wealthy enough to enjoy such privilege: the Romans built villas along the river's fertile banks, and it later became a rural escape route for the monarchy who, from Henry II onwards, have generally preferred Windsor Castle as their principal place of residence. The area was again favoured during the Victorian era, when wealthy industrialists built Neoclassical villas along the river banks; it was also much frequented by day-tripping Londoners – nearly seven thousand people took the train to Henley to enjoy the 1888 regatta. The towns and villages of the Thames Valley comprise what is still the most prized part of London's commuter belt, lending parts of the area an exclusive and sometimes snobbish air. More positively, the not-in-my-back-yard mentality has ensured that the region remains largely unblighted by development, despite its proximity to the metropolis, and the countryside around Silchester and Hambleden is beautifully unspoiled.

The first walk in this chapter leads through expansive **Windsor Great Park**, dominated by the imposing profile of its medieval castle. The second walk takes you along the **Thames Towpath** from Henley to the picturesque Chilterns village of Hambleden for lunch, and on via wooded hills to Marlow, another prosperous little Thames-side town. The final route lies to the south of the river, running from Stratfield Mortimer to the strikingly evocative remains of the Roman settlement of Calleva, just outside the village of **Silchester**, and then across country to Bramley.

This is an easy area to access by **train**: services are regular and relatively efficient. Trains for Eton Riverside, the departure point for the Windsor walk, depart from **Waterloo**, calling at Clapham Junction and Richmond, and also from Paddington via Slough. For Henley, services leave from **Paddington**, with additional stops at Ealing Broadway and Slough. Trains also leave from Paddington for Stratfield Mortimer, the stop for the Silchester walk, calling at Ealing Broadway and Slough. The Windsor walk is a good option for **drivers** – the Henley one is the trickiest, as there are no direct trains from Marlow to Henley. For all these routes, **start walking** around 11am to reach the recommended place for lunch.

Windsor Great Park

Eton Riverside to Windsor Great Park

Distance and difficulty: 20km; moderate.
Trains: London Waterloo to Eton Riverside (every 30min; 50min)
or London Paddington to Eton Riverside (every 30min; 40min);
return from Eton Riverside to London Waterloo (every 30min;
50min) or London Paddington (every 30min; 45min).
Map: OS Landranger 175: *Reading & Windsor*; OS Explorer 160:
Windsor and Weybridge.

Windsor Great Park, measuring some 24km in circumference, is too extensive to be a park in the ordinary sense of the word, and while there are some formal gardens and graceful avenues of trees, large sections remain wooded and relatively wild, and parts are given over to farmland. Giant oaks and beeches flourish, some standing solitary and some in thick clusters – several of the oaks date back to the Norman conquest. Medieval Windsor Castle, one of the major seats of the royal family, is superbly theatrical, if slightly Disneyfied, while the grace-and-favour houses scattered throughout the park certainly give you a sense of how the other half live – if you enjoy seeing the upper classes at play, the sight of the polo ground might provide some amusement. The best **time to visit** is late May and early June, when the rhododendrons and azaleas are in bloom. Lunch and snacks can be bought at the *Savill Garden Tearoom* but it's no great shakes, so you might prefer to bring a **picnic**.

Parts of the castle are open to the public, though these aren't described in detail here, as you're unlikely to be able to visit the castle and do this longish walk in one day.

Some background

Windsor Castle lies at the northeastern edge of Windsor on a low mound, which gives it a commanding position above the town and park. William the Conqueror acquired the surrounding forest for hunting, and established the castle as an important residence of the English sovereigns, which it remains. William replaced an earlier wooden keep with a stone circuit wall. The castle's first round tower was built by Henry III around 1272, but Edward III reconstructed it in about 1344 as a meeting place for the newly established Knights of the Garter. Subsequent additions were made over the centuries until the 1820s, when over-zealous restoration by George IV diminished the castle's presence, giving it a toy-town look that chimes with the heavily heritage-bound atmosphere of Windsor itself. The Chapel of St George with-

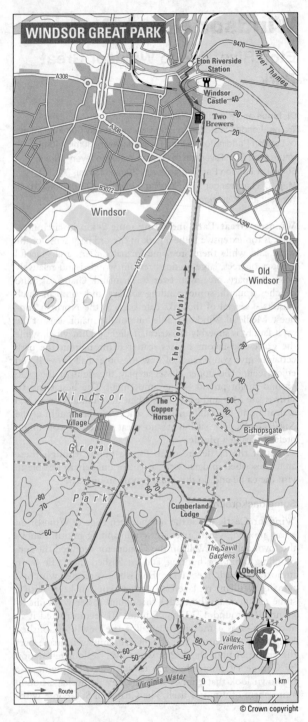

in the castle walls, however, is one of the finest examples of Perpendicular architecture in England, and ranks second only to Westminster Abbey as a royal mausoleum.

Since the time of William the Conqueror, the castle has played an important role in English history. Most dramatically perhaps, it was seized in 1642 by the **Parliamentary army** under Colonel Venn, who desecrated the chapel and killed the park's deer. Charles I was imprisoned in the castle in 1647, and taken from there to Whitehall, where he was executed. His body was returned to Windsor in a coffin, and was buried without ceremony.

The most significant event in the castle's recent history was the **fire** during the queen's "annus horribilis" of 1992, which gutted many of the State Apartments; the royals were inadequately insured, so the queen was obliged to fork out for half the £50 million repair bill, as the nation expressed its reluctantance at shouldering the entire burden.

Windsor Great Park is open daily from dawn till dusk; free.
Windsor Castle is open daily March–Oct 9.45am–5.15pm;
Nov–Feb 9.45am–4.15pm; £11.50; ⓦ www.royal.gov.uk.

The **park** itself was enclosed for the hunting of boar and deer in the thirteenth century. In 1580, Lord Burleigh ordered the planting of trees within the park to replenish timber stocks following the war with Spain. Charles II planted the Long Walk, which links the castle and the park, in 1680. George III was confined at Windsor during his "madness", diagnosed in the twentieth century as a rare metabolic disorder, famously jumping from his carriage to address an oak tree as the King of Prussia. The unstable monarch, known as Farmer George, was responsible for introducing agriculture to the park – farming and forestry interests were later developed by Prince Albert, and remain a significant part of the park's profile. More whimsically, the park is said to have been haunted for the last thousand years by **Herne the Hunter**, who wears the antlers of a stag and rides a black stallion with a pack of black hounds at his feet; he appears when there is trouble ahead, then gallops through the park and melts into the air.

Getting started

0.5km

Exit **Eton Riverside station** and turn right towards Windsor town centre, then take the first left towards the information office and the castle, which you'll see rising up on the left-hand side. Continue up the hill and round the flanks of the castle, then head straight up the High Street, following signs for the Long Walk. At the end of the main street, turn slightly to the left up Park Street. You'll see the rose-covered *Two Brewers* pub on the left; go through the gates just beyond and into the park, then turn right for the Long Walk.

The Long Walk and Savill Garden

6.5km

The Long Walk, laid out in the time of Charles II and William III, runs in a straight sweep, lined with plane and horse chestnut trees and bookended by Windsor Castle and a bombastic copper statue of George III on horseback, known as the Copper Horse. The walk crosses Albert Road (the A308), but is otherwise uninterrupted, except for the gate you pass through to enter the deer park. At the end of the long paved path, climb up the little mound to the **Copper Horse**; behind it, follow the wide grassy path which runs between hedgerows and curves round to the left, eventually entering a patch of oak woodland.

Head through the oak woodland to emerge onto a paved path. Turn left and almost immediately right, following the signs to handsome **Cumberland Lodge**, built in the time of Oliver Cromwell and named for the odious Duke of Cumberland (see opposite). It's now a conference centre, set up with royal approval to facilitate discussion about the Commonwealth from a Christian perspective. Just before you get to the lodge, take the path which curves round it to the left. Beyond the lodge, turn left and, at the crossroads beyond, turn right onto the paved path. You pass some tile-hung cottages, then come to an orange-brick gatehouse, **Cumberland Gate**.

Go through the gate and turn left onto the paved path, along the polo ground, passing a beautiful dove-grey Georgian house on the left, festooned with clematis and roses, and go through walkways of rhododendrons and azaleas. Continue to follow the signs along the sinuous path leading towards Savill Garden – you'll see the walled gardens on the right-hand side, and a huge greenhouse. The path curves round to the right; follow it for another 250m to the entrance to the garden and tea-room, which lies on the right. **Savill Garden** (daily: March–Oct 10am–6pm; Nov–Feb 10am–4pm; April & May £5, June–Oct £4.50, Nov–March £2.75) is a woodland garden, begun in the 1930s, which incorporates herbaceous borders, rose gardens, peat beds and a bog garden, as well as umpteen rhododendrons and azaleas.

....

The purpose-built *Savill Garden Tearoom* is functional
but uninspiring, with a touch of the motorway caff about it.
The food – sandwiches, soups and cakes – is a little stodgy
and overpriced, though the large windows allow free views
of the garden itself.

....

Valley Gardens

5km

To continue the walk, take a right out of the tearoom and gardens. After 250m you'll see a huge **obelisk** on the right-hand side, raised by George II for his son, William, Duke of Cumberland. This overblown monument recalls the commander who became known as "the butcher" for his grotesquely cruel treatment of soldiers and civilians following the Battle of Culloden in 1746. In contrast, **Obelisk Pond** lies on the right, surrounded by sweet chestnuts and rhododendrons and edged by yellow irises.

Some 200m beyond the pond, you come to a junction. Turn right into a birch wood and continue until you emerge at the bottom of a polo field, then carry on for 500m along the polo field, keeping to the right. Where you come to a T-junction, turn left, heading down the road into the **Valley Gardens**, which comprise flowering trees, shrubs and hardy plants. At the junction, head for 1.5km towards Blacknest Gate, crossing **Virginia Water** twice. Just before you reach the little pink gatehouse, there's a riding track to the right-hand side which, though churned by hooves, saves you walking on the road. Follow the track through the wood for 1.5km.

Duke's Lane

3km

Turn right where the path joins the paved **Duke's Lane**. From this point, you are back in quietly dramatic open parkland. You reach a red-brick cottage called "The Hollies" on the right – go straight ahead at the junction here. The road is crossed by a couple of other narrower roads; keep going straight on and you'll eventually see Windsor Castle ahead, with the Copper Horse to the right. At the end of Duke's Lane, turn right through the gates into the deer park; after 600m you reach the foot of the mound surmounted by the Copper Horse.

Back to Windsor

5km

From here, rejoin the **Long Walk** to head back up to Windsor. Towards evening, the great trees lining the walk throw long shadows, the deer are more in evidence, and the imposing asymmetry of Windsor Castle forms a fine backdrop. Just out of the gates of the park, on the right, the welcoming *Two Brewers* is an excellent place to stop for a pint before you head home.

The Thames Towpath and the Chiltern Way

Henley to Marlow via Hambleden

Distance and difficulty: 14.5km; moderate.
Train: London Paddington to Henley (hourly; 55min); Marlow to London Paddington (hourly; 1hr).
Map: OS Landranger 175: *Reading & Windsor*; OS Explorer 171 and 172: *Chiltern Hills West* and *Chiltern Hills East*.

This satisfying walk runs between the affluent Thames towns of **Henley** and **Marlow**, passing through the Chilterns village of **Hambleden** en route, which makes a good stop for a pub lunch. The route from Henley runs along the east bank of the **Thames**, past rowing clubs housed in neat pavilions and elegant villas with wooden boathouses. The crowds of dog-walkers and families thin out as you walk further north up the Thames, until the only sounds are the thwack of swans' wings on the water and the shouts of the rowing coaches who cycle up and down the path, bellowing at rowers in the passing racing boats. At **Hambleden Lock** you cross the Thames over a roaring weir to **Mill's End**. From here the route leaves the river and runs across meadows to the unspoilt little village of **Hambleden**. Beyond Hambleden, a steep climb takes you into the Chilterns, after which the route – now following the **Chilterns Way** – levels out, taking you across farmland and downs and through two dense stretches of woodland: **Homefield** and **Davenport woods**. From there you descend, via minor roads, into **Marlow**.

You'll need to buy a single ticket from London to Henley, and another single back from Marlow, as the stations are on different lines.

Henley to Hambleden Lock
4.5km

Coming out of **Henley station**, turn right and walk for 50m towards the *Imperial Hotel*. Turn right at the hotel, and head down to the river, then turn left towards the eighteenth-century *Angel* pub; if you fancy a cuppa before you start, try the *Henley Tearooms*, on the left on the way to the pub. At the *Angel*, cross the bridge and continue 50m down the road, then turn left, following the Thames Towpath sign towards Hambleden Lock.

The **Thames Towpath** runs down the wide and grassy east bank of the river. This is where crowds gather for the **Henley Regatta**, which runs from the last Wednesday in June to the

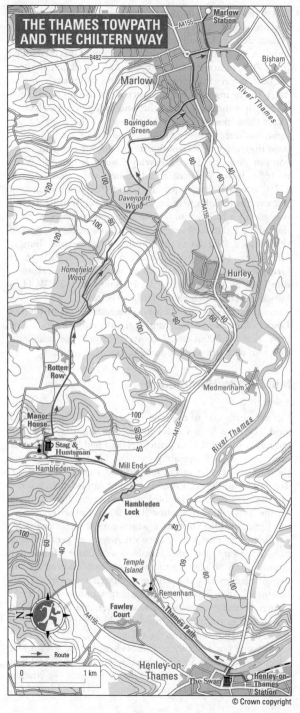

THE THAMES TOWPATH AND THE CHILTERN WAY 157

first week in July. The regatta's first incarnation was as the Oxford and Cambridge boat race, which ran between Hambleden Lock and Henley Bridge in 1829, but which was soon moved to London; Henley Regatta itself was established in 1839. A bizarre fixture in the British social and sporting calendar, the regatta's principal attraction these days is not so much the racing itself but the spectacle of legions of drunken posh people mooning each other and falling into the river.

Less than 2km beyond Henley, just off the route to the right, you'll see a cluster of houses and a church which comprise the village of **Remenham** – to the left across the river you can glimpse red-brick **Fawley Court**, designed by Wren in 1684; James Wyatt made additions to the house in the 1770s, at which time Capability Brown designed the gardens. Just over half a kilometre beyond the house, **Temple Island** is home to a little white temple, designed by James Wyatt as the fishing lodge for Fawley Court; it now marks the start of the Henley Regatta course. Some 700m beyond Temple Island on the opposite bank stands the village of **Greenlands**, home to a gleaming white Neoclassical mansion built by the newsagent W. H. Smith in 1853. W. H. is buried in Hambleden churchyard (see below).

Seven hundred metres beyond Greenlands is **Hambleden Lock**: follow the public footpath sign to cross the lock. The path leads for 300m along the weir, through the middle of the river, with the water thundering down to the right.

Mill End to Hambleden

1.5km

On the north side of the river is the tiny settlement of **Mill End**. There has been a mill here since at least 1086; the present mill, a substantial but plain clapboard building with a slate roof, only stopped operating in 1952. Go past the mill and the attractive cluster of cottages beyond and on to the road. Turn right on the road then left almost immediately, following the road sign to Hambleden. At the right-hand turning for the minor road to Rotten Row, 300m further on, follow the signed **public footpath**, which runs through the fields parallel to the road you've been on. Ahead are gentle rolling hills, topped by woodland; Hambleden's **Manor House** (see opposite) can be seen up to your right, while ahead are the orange-tiled roofs and square grey church tower of the village itself. After 500m the path emerges onto a little track; turn right and continue for a few metres, and then take the signed public footpath on the left, which runs for another 500m through meadows to the village.

You come out at a tiny arched bridge over the stream that edges **Hambleden**, a neat little village of red-brick and flint houses surrounded by profuse cottage gardens. Go straight ahead through the village to the mainly Norman **Church of**

St Mary the Virgin. Inside, don't miss the alabaster and marble memorial to Cope and Martha D'Oyley (died 1633 and 1618 respectively) and their five sons and five daughters. Two of the sons wear Royalist garb; the rest wear Puritan outfits. The children who predeceased their father hold skulls, a macabre touch intensified by the masterful depiction of each member of the family – it's thought they are actual, rather than idealized, portraits.

Continue along the road through the village to reach the **pub**.

....

The friendly and bustling *Stag & Huntsman* pub
(℡01491/571227) serves good bar food, real ale on
handpump, and farm cider, and there's a large garden at the
back, though it gets packed on sunny days.

....

The Chiltern Way to Marlow

6km

From Hambleden, the route ascend into the Chilterns, and picks up the **Chilterns Way**, which takes you all the way to the outskirts of Marlow. Coming out of the pub, turn right and go up the private road ahead of you. Past the pub car park, take the first right, where you see a public footpath sign. Go up this track; after 150m there's a turn-off to the left, marked with a yellow arrow on a post and signposted as the Chiltern Way. Go up the skinny path which leads steeply through a field, passing the **Manor House** on the left. The house's plain brick Georgian facade conceals an early seventeenth-century interior; Charles I stayed here in 1646 during his flight from Oxford to St Albans, just prior to his imprisonment. At the top of the hill, continue along the path through the woods for 400m. When you're nearly through the wood you'll see a track to the left and a footpath sign ahead – follow the footpath sign which points ahead through the fields, leaving the patch of woodland.

Four hundred metres beyond the woodland, the path comes out onto a track; go straight ahead towards the flint farm buildings that comprise the hamlet of **Rotten Row**. After 200m you come onto the curve of a road; turn left towards the buildings of Rotten Row, passing the farm on your left and a pond on the right. Go straight ahead, following the Chilterns Way sign into the field. At the end of the field, with the woods ahead of you, turn right onto a minor road. Ignore the public footpath sign to the left after 150m and carry on down the road for another 200m to reach a second public footpath sign on the left, with Woodside House to the left.

The path leads into the beech woods, skirting round the edge of **Homefield Hall**. The path is a little faint here – it descends the hill, via a small stile, to join a track after 250m;

turn right here and continue through **Homefield Wood**, a National Trust nature reserve. After 650m you come out onto a minor road; turn right along the road for a few metres, then left, following the Chilterns Way signs. Carry on for 500m across the grassy downland till you reach **Davenport Wood**. Go straight ahead, following the Chilterns Way signs and climbing steeply up the hill – the path is rather faint, but bear in mind that 200m into the wood you need to cross the road that runs through it. Once across the road, the path continues straight ahead, though again it's rather indistinct – the white arrows painted on the trees every 50m or so should keep you on course. Carry on through the woods, following both the Chiltern Way signs and the white arrows. After 600m you emerge from the woods, with some orange-brick houses ahead of you.

Into Marlow

2.5km

You come out at the village of **Bovingdon Green** – rather than crossing the green, turn right past the row of red-brick cottages. Walk down the minor road for just over a kilometre, with villas and cottages lining the road as you walk through the outskirts of Marlow. The road, signed after 600m as **Spinfield Lane**, leads downhill into **Marlow** and joins a main road at the bottom of the hill. Turn left, and look out on the left for a white villa with pointy Gothick windows. Shelley and his wife Mary lived here from 1817 to 1818 – it was here that Mary, at the tender age of 21, wrote *Frankenstein*.

Some 650m metres beyond the point where you turned left along the main road, you reach a roundabout. Turn right here, following the signs to the station, down Marlow's busy High Street, lined with Georgian and Victorian buildings. At the end of the High Street, at another roundabout, turn left onto Station Road. Carry on for 650m; **Marlow station** is on the right, just beyond the *Marlow Donkey* pub.

Roman Silchester

Stratfield Mortimer to Bramley, via Calleva

Distance and difficulty: 13km; moderate.
Trains: Paddington to Mortimer via Reading (every 30min; 50min); return from Bramley to Paddington via Reading (every 30min; 1hr).
Map: OS Landranger 175: *Reading & Windsor*; OS Explorer 159: *Reading*.

This extremely pretty and satisfying walk runs along footpaths and country lanes from the hamlet of **Stratfield Mortimer** to the picturesque remains of the Roman town of **Calleva** – a stately ring of defensive walls and a well-preserved amphitheatre, one of only sixteen built in Roman Britain. There's a convenient if slightly mediocre **lunch** stop at the *Calleva Arms* in the nearby village of **Silchester**, though in good weather you might prefer to have a picnic at

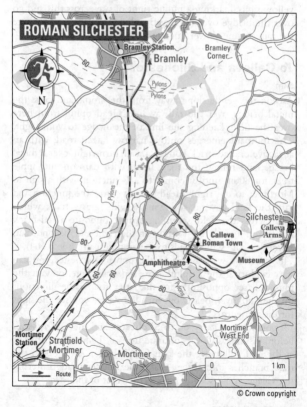

© Crown copyright

Calleva itself, where there are plenty of scenic spots. From the ruins, the route leads across country to the station at **Bramley**.

Along Foudry Brook

1.5km

From **Mortimer station**, turn left down Station Road; when you come to the junction at the end of the road, turn left. Continue up this road for 200m, then turn left at the green metal "byway" sign and follow the path past the church.

Beyond the church, at the end of the track, turn right, keeping **Foudry Brook** to your right. After 500m there's a junction – cross over Foudry Book using the metal bridge and then continue along the path on the other side of the brook. Walk along the brook for a kilometre, until you see a small wooden stile on the left. Cross the stile and go across the field to the brook (there isn't a proper path at this point), turn right and continue along the field with the brook immediately to your left. At the end of the field, cross the wooden stile with the yellow sign, then carry on over the small stream. At the end of the next field there's a stile with yellow signs, marking a public right of way; cross this and go over the bridge over Foudry Brook – it's at the point where the railway line, power lines and brook almost converge.

To Calleva and Silchester

5km

Ascend the gentle slope away from the brook, and cross the metal bridge over the railway line. Head uphill from here over the field, keeping the line of the hedge to your right. The footpath emerges onto a narrow tarred road, with an attractive orange-brick cottage ahead; turn right, over a metal bridge, and follow the road, lined with damson and apple trees, for 800m until it comes to a T-junction, with a sign to Mortimer to the right. Head straight across the junction and into the field beyond, following a wide, grassy track which leads across the field, rejoining tarmac opposite a red-brick house. You'll see a red postbox on the right and, beyond that, a wooden gate which leads to the amphitheatre (see p.164).

If you don't want to go to the pub in Silchester you can start exploring the amphitheatre and walls here, or visit the museum (see opposite) – for the latter, follow the directions for the pub given below but turn left where you see the signs for the museum.

If you want to carry on to **Silchester** and the *Calleva Arms* before visiting Calleva, continue up Wall Lane, then turn left at the end, following the sign for Silchester. After 800m the road branches into three – take the middle route. Entering the village, you'll see the **pub** to the right of the road.

Calleva museum and site

2.5km

From the pub, retrace your steps for 600m, then follow the wooden sign to the right to the excellent **Calleva Museum**

The life and death of Calleva

No one knows why, when the Romans withdrew from Britain at the beginning of the fifth century, **Calleva** was abandoned, unlike similar towns such as Winchester and Canterbury. Whatever the reasons, the fact that the site was never developed means that its layout remains spectacularly intact. The walls describe an irregular hexagon and were built in the third century when, like many Western European towns, Silchester must have felt the threat of barbarian invasion. Traces of Roman roads radiate out from the main gates; these would have cut through thick forest to link the town with Winchester, London and other lesser settlements.

At the heart of the town lay the **forum**, a great open square lined with two-storey colonnaded public buildings and shops; the town's principal roads converged here. Along the forum's west side was the **basilica**, an aisled hall, thought to have been 25m high and constructed using marble from Italy – it was here that taxes were collected and justice was meted out. Just southeast of the forum sat a small fourth-century **church**, built after 313 AD, when Christianity was no longer a proscribed religion. The town's other major buildings included an elaborate bathhouse with an exercise court, three temples and an official guesthouse.

There were only around eighty houses of any significance at Calleva, their scant number and modest though graceful mosaics and frescoes suggesting that the town was not populous or extravagantly wealthy. Latin as opposed to Old English, was written and spoken, and the thoroughly Romanized British inhabitants would have worn imported jewellery, drunk imported wine and cooked with imported oil. Calleva served as the market town for the surrounding area, and there was some commercial activity: metal-working, pottery-making, glass- and lead-production, carpentry, milling and brewing.

There is some evidence – such as the apparently deliberate filling up of the town's wells with rubble – that suggests that Calleva was systematically evacuated and then destroyed, perhaps because of the political rise of Dorchester-on-Thames in the post-Roman period. Beyond that, it's impossible to trace the story of the town's demise and eventual abandonment.

(9am–dusk; free). Housed in a green, shed-like building, the museum uses interpretive panels and artists' impressions of Calleva to trace the history of the site from its beginnings as a pre-Roman tribal centre.

From the museum, turn left to follow the bridleway to the Roman walls – you can retrace your steps and go back along the road, but this way is prettier. You'll pass red-brick cottages on the left-hand side, and cross a wooden stile. Ignore the little stile to the left, and continue down the narrow path, then pass through the wooden gate to take the **Roman Town Trail**, which circles round the walls.

Turning to the **left** here leads you directly to the amphitheatre and church, and the route on to Bramley. A path to the right cuts straight across the site, though there's nothing to see in what was once the beating heart of Calleva, since the excavated buildings have been reburied to protect them from the elements. It's more fun to walk along the walls, however, which are punctuated by lofty oak and ash trees.

From the top of the walls you can appreciate the scope and symmetry of the site, as well as its tactical significance – it occupies high ground, with sweeping views to the south and east. The **walls** themselves, striped in flint and mortar, stand as high as 4.5m in some places, their expensive materials reflecting Calleva's importance. A number of gateways stud the 2.5-kilometre circumference; a pair of human skulls were found outside the north gate, which guarded the route towards Dorchester-on-Thames – it's thought that severed heads on poles stood grisly guard to either side of the gateway.

Having circled the northern part of the walls, you'll see some flint and wood farm buildings and the church to your right. Follow the path which leads to the left, down from the walls – which are particularly impressive at this point – to a wooden stile and gate. Another stile with a plank bridge leads up to the road; turn right towards the amphitheatre, which is tucked in the trees beyond a wooden fence.

The amphitheatre

Built in 55–75 AD in earth and timber, and rebuilt in stone in the third century, Calleva's **amphitheatre**, ringed around with oak, silver birch, holly and ash, lacks the grandeur of those in mainland Europe, though it's still a dramatic-looking place, with steeply raked concave walls and an oval arena. Public entertainments took place here on holidays and festivals and are thought to have featured riding displays, animal hunts and wild beast shows rather than gladiatorial contests. A long period of obscurity followed the amphitheatre's glory days: an eighteenth-century observer, the antiquary William Stukely, wrote that the overgrown site had "from times immemorial been a yard for cattle and a watering pond".

St Mary the Virgin Church

Head out of the amphitheatre through the wooden gates, following the curve of the road, with a red letter box to the left and Manor Farmhouse to the right, to reach **St Mary the Virgin Church**, a charming thirteenth-century building with a low bell tower, partly built using stone from Calleva; a column from one of the Roman temples lies just to the west of the church. Outside its east end are two fourteenth-century coffin lids, carved with portrait busts and foliated crosses. Inside the church, look for the slender effigy of **Eleanor Baynard**, wearing a wimple, with a dog at her feet and two winged angels at her head. Baynard was a wealthy resident of Silchester who obtained permission to worship at a private oratory in her house in 1348, the first year of the Black Death. (The proliferation of mid-fourteenth-century names in the list of clergy in the church reflects the dreadful toll taken by the Black Death.) Eleanor may have commissioned the remodelling of the church – the south aisle was rebuilt to accommodate large Gothic windows with intricate tracery. The fine early sixteenth-century **screen**, carved from gleaming dark oak, has an exuberant frieze depicting feathered angels, a pomegranate and a Tudor rose.

Across country to Bramley

4km

Opposite the driveway to St Mary's, go up the wooden steps through the hedgerow; turn right into the field, and head down towards the line of trees. At the bottom of the field, turn left and follow the path round the field. When you get to the far corner, go straight ahead; you'll see a wooden sign telling you to keep dogs on a lead, and white arrows painted on the trees. Head straight on to where the path dips slightly into a field, curve round the field to the right, and then go straight ahead. At this point the path broadens out, becoming wide and grassy, and joins a little track at the end of the field.

Turn left and continue for a few metres, then go right over a stile, with a copse on the left. Head up the field and keep the fence to the left; go over the stile straight ahead (ignoring the one to the right) and cross a concrete bridge – carry on until you reach a stile to the left which leads onto the road, with a red-brick house on the left-hand side.

Follow the road as it curves round to the right – ignore the left-hand turn to the pub. After 750m you come to a T-junction: take the left-hand route to Bramley. Some 800m further on, take the turning on the right, just before the red-brick railway bridge. Heading down the road you'll see tall pylons marching towards an electricity substation to the right of the road. Entering the village of **Bramley**, look out for the quirky barn to the left, resting on stone toadstools which protect its contents from rodents. Just beyond the barn, turn left towards Bramley train station; the *Bramley Inn* is on the left-hand side and the station just beyond to the right.

7

The Chilterns and Blenheim

F lanking London's northwestern edges, the **Chiltern Hills** are part of an extensive range of chalk uplands that run from Wiltshire in the west all the way to Yorkshire in the north. The Chilterns are the most dramatic part of these uplands within easy reach of London, rising on their western side to a high, steeply shelving escarpment offering panoramic views west and backed by the characteristic beech woodlands which thrive in the hills' chalky soil. Beyond the escarpment, the gentle Oxfordshire countryside undulates away towards the Cotswolds, providing the setting for **Bleinheim Palace**, one of the greatest of all English stately homes.

The first of the walks in this chapter heads out from the commuter town of Amersham, through the Chilterns via the attractive **Misbourne Valley**, to the village of Chalfont St Giles. The second walk starts in Wendover and leads west to the Chiltern's highest viewpoint, Coombe Hill, before descending into the **Chequers Estate**, the British prime minister's country retreat. The third walk follows the Ridgeway trail from Tring to **Ivinghoe Beacon**, the second highest of the Chiltern viewpoints, before looping back through beech woods to Tring. Beyond the Chilterns, in the heart of the Oxfordshire countryside, the last of the walks in this chapter makes a circuit of the **Blenheim Estate**, and also includes a detour to the Roman villa remains at North Leigh.

The Chilterns walks in this chapter are easily and cheaply reached from **Marylebone** train station; the walk from Amersham can also be reached by tube (Metropolitan Line) and is covered on a zone 1–6 Travelcard (though you'll need to ask for a special free, extension ticket that covers this station). Blenheim is a little more expensive to reach; trains depart from **Paddington** station. All four walks in this chapter are circular, and therefore convenient if you're **driving**. Aim to start walking by around 11am for all these routes.

The Misbourne Valley

Amersham to Chalfont St Giles and back

Distance and difficulty: 16km; moderate.
Train: Marylebone to Amersham either by overground train (every 30min; 30min) or tube (Metropolitan Line); return from Amersham to Marylebone (every 30min; 30min).
Map: OS Landranger 165 and 175: *Aylesbury & Leighton Buzzard*; and *Reading & Windsor* OS Explorer 172: *Chiltern Hills East*.

This easily accessible walk, reachable from London either by train or tube, leads from Amersham to Chalfont St Giles and back again, following the **Misbourne Valley** as it cuts through the Chilterns. Starting at the station in **Amersham-on-the-Hill**, the route begins by descending into the pretty medieval country town of **Amersham**. Past Amersham, the walk follows a ridge of the Chilterns above the Misbourne Valley into **Chalfont St Giles**. Centred on an attractive village green, Chalfont boasts the cottage (now a museum) that John Milton lived in while he completed *Paradise Lost*, as well as plenty of pubs for **lunch** – the pick of the crop is *Merlin's Cave*, right on the village green. The **return route** back to Amersham again follows the River Misbourne, but this time along the valley floor, offering a fresh perspective on the chalky surrounding hills.

Getting started

1km

Exit the train station into **Amersham-on-the-Hill** and head down to the junction by the *Iron Horse* pub. Turn left onto the main road (A416) and head under the railway bridge and downhill towards Amersham Old Town. From here you can see over the rooftops of the Victorian cottages that line the road and across the valley to the farmland and wooded hilltops through which the walk will take you.

Some 200m beyond the bridge and just before Parsonage Place, a short row of houses set back from the main road, take the well-marked public footpath which goes around the back of the houses and up into **Parsonage Wood**. Keeping close to the easterly edges of the wood, the track rises sharply for the first 50m or so, then levels off as it heads through the heart of the wood and out to Rectory Hill Road after roughly 300m.

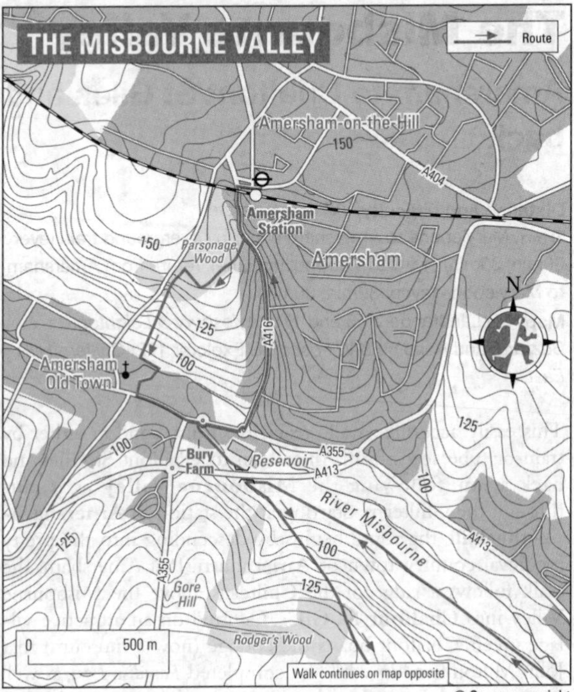
THE MISBOURNE VALLEY
Route
Amersham-on-the-Hill
150
A404
Amersham Station
150
Parsonage Wood
Amersham
N
125
A416
100
Amersham Old Town
125
100
Bury Farm
Reservoir
A355
A413
100
River Misbourne
A413
125
100
A355
Gore Hill
125
0
500 m
Rodger's Wood
Walk continues on map opposite

© Crown copyright

Amersham Old Town

0.5km

Just before you reach the road, bear left and head downhill on a tarred path out of the wood and over grassland to **Amersham Old Town**, which sits on the banks of the River Misbourne below, its centre marked by the tower of St Mary's parish church. At the bottom of the hill, the track ends at a T-junction before a high red-brick wall; to your left is the old **cemetery**. Take the footpath that leads to the left, then, a few metres further on, cross the **River Misbourne**, little more than a babbling brook at this point, via the tiny stone bridge to your right. This brings you to the end of the cul-de-sac on which **St Mary's Church** sits. Though the original church dates from the thirteenth century, much of what you see today – including the flint facing, the stair-turrret and much of the interior – are part of a heavy-handed late-Victorian restoration; it's a handsome building, nonetheless, in an attractive setting at the heart of the old town.

Turn left into the churchyard, 100m from the bridge, and follow the path through to the aptly named **Broadway**, the old town's main drag. Here, tiny timber-framed and brick-fronted seventeenth-century cottages line the wide main street. Just to your right, at the end of Broadway, is the red-brick **Market Hall**, topped by a wooden bell-turret.

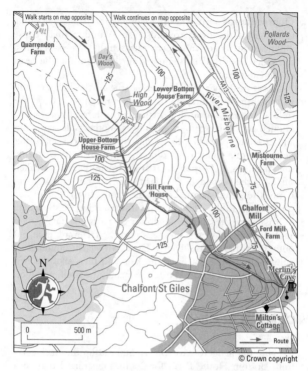

Turn left and follow Broadway for 200m, heading out of town to the roundabout by Tesco. Just beyond the round-about, metres from the start of London Road West and just before **Bury Cottage**, on the opposite side of the road, turn right into **Bury Farm**. Note that the public footpath sign is lost in the trees to walkers heading in this direction; you'll only spot it once you're at the farm entrance. Bear left to head behind Bury Cottage and over a stile into a field between a reservoir to your left and the A413 to your right.

Amersham to Upper Bottom House Farm

3.5km

At the far side of the field, head through the tunnel under the A413 and up into farmland. In the hedgerow on the right, 50m or so from the tunnel, is a stile; cross this and head through two fields and over another stile, climbing steadily and aiming for the left-hand side of **Rodger's Wood**, which runs along the brow of Gore Hill, overlooking the valley. At the edge of the wood, cross another stile and take the path on the opposite side, which cuts through the woods to reach a second stile after 100m, at the edge of a field. Cross this stile and head diagonally across the field to the end of the hedgerow on your right, over the access road to

Quarrendon Farm, and on, following the hedgerows along the edge of the fields towards Day's Wood, a small copse 300m ahead. There are superb views from here back across the valley floor to Amersham and further west into the heart of the Chilterns.

Just before **Day's Wood**, cross a stile in the hedgerow to your right and go into the field with a pylon in it. Cross the field diagonally, aiming a little to the left of the pylon. Hidden in the hedgerow opposite is another stile; cross this and continue downhill, to the far right-hand corner of this field. To your right, nestled at the bottom of two steeply shelving hills, is **Upper Bottom House Farm**, so called since it's the second of two farms on Bottom House Farm Lane; the other farm, Lower Bottom House Farm (see p.174), is off to the left, down towards the River Misbourne.

Cross the stile and head down towards the farm, over another stile and down the steps into the farmyard, then out onto **Bottom House Farm Lane**, with farm buildings to either side. Turn right onto the lane and then take the first left at the end of it, just before the farmhouse itself, uphill on a dirt track.

Chalfont St Giles

3km

Keeping the hedgerow to your right, head up the track away from Bottom House Farm for 200m, then turn left onto a minor track just before an enclosed area of woodland. Follow this track uphill to reach Hill House Farm, then go along the lane ahead (Hill Farm Lane) through Rushcroft Wood and then downhill into **Chalfont St Giles**. You emerge on Mill Lane, at the edge of the village. Cross this and head straight on down Dodds Lane, which becomes Silver Hill and leads after 750m to the attractive little High Street and village green, surrounded by seventeenth-century timber- and brick-built cottages. Behind the High Street, the village's heavily restored medieval flint church rises above the houses.

Right on the village green, the *Merlin's Cave* pub (daily noon–3pm; ☎ 01494/875101) serves good, if predictable, pub-grub plus Sunday roasts. To its right, also overlooking the green, is the pleasant *Tea Time Coffee Shop*.

What brings most visitors to Chalfont St Giles is **Milton's Cottage** (March–Oct Tues–Sun 10am–1pm & 2–6pm; £2.50), in which the poet sought refuge from plague-stricken London in 1665 as a guest of Thomas Ellwood. Milton completed *Paradise Lost* here, and it was during the same stay that Ellwood suggested to him the idea of *Paradise Regained*. The red-brick and tiled cottage now contains a modest little **museum** devoted to Milton's life and works, including first editions of his poems. The house is a few hundred metres uphill from the village green, on Dean Way, the continuation of the High Street.

Chalfont St Giles and Lower Bottom House Farm

2.5km

The route back to Amersham is easy to follow. From the village green, take the public footpath that begins on a private lane just to the right of **Silver Hill**, the road you came down to reach the High Street. At the end of this lane, 300m from the High Street, the track continues straight on into woodland and comes out a further 200m into the end of a cul-de-sac, which in turn leads out onto **Mill Lane**, at the point at which it crosses the River Misbourne; Ford Mill Farm stands on one side of the lane, Chalfont Mill on the other, with the ford itself running over the lane just a few metres to the right of the path – a deluge in winter, but often little more than a trickle in the drier summer months.

Just to the left of the mill, at the point at which you meet Mill Lane, the lane bends right to flank the river, then left 50m further on. Go straight on, following the lane parallel to the river and passing to the left of the mill to rejoin the public footpath at the waymarkers by the second bend. Again, the track heads through the trees, their branches here arching over the path to make a shady avenue, dappled with light, for the next kilometre or so. The River Misbourne flows some 500m to your right – you'll catch glimpses of it intermittently for the rest of the walk, though you'll see little of it at this stage – and there are views across the Misbourne Valley and over to Pollards Wood on the hillside opposite.

Lower Bottom House Farm to Amersham train station

5.5km

The path through the avenue of trees ends at a stile. Head over it into a field and from here continue in a northerly direction crossing fields and stiles for a little over 4km to return to Amersham Old Town at Bury Farm and Cottage. Two fields on from the avenue of trees you'll recross Bottom House Farm Lane a few hundred metres below **Lower Bottom House Farm** – its attractive dark-wood and red-tiled barns stand at the top of the fields to your left.

From here it's field, stile, field, stile all the way back to the tunnel under the A413. With the wooded hills east of Amersham rising above you to the right and the hills along which you walked earlier looming up to the left, this is a much more enclosed route than the walk out to Chalfont St Giles. The going is much easier, too, as the path not only follows the flat valley floor, but also largely crosses pasture rather than arable land. You briefly rejoin the **Misbourne** a couple of fields beyond Bottom House Farm Lane, and then pass by a copse before **Rodger's Wood** comes into view on the hill-top to your left and **Amersham-on-the-Hill** rises above the valley floor ahead.

Seven fields and umpteen stiles beyond Bottom House Farm Lane, you reach the tunnel under the A413, which leads out to the field before Bury Farm; head back through the farm and down its drive to London Road West. From here, just to the left of **Bury Cottage**, you can retrace your steps back via Amersham Old Town to return to Amersham station. Alternatively, for a more direct route back to the station, turn right then first left at the roundabout at the far end of the Tesco car park to head up **Station Road** (the A416).

The Northern Chilterns

Wendover to Chequers via Coombe Hill

Distance and difficulty: 15km; moderate.
Train: Marylebone to Wendover (1–2 hourly; 45min); return from Wendover to Marylebone (1–2 hourly; 45min).
Map: OS Landranger 165: *Aylesbury & Leighton Buzzard*; OS Explorer 181: *Chiltern Hills North*.

This fine circular walk begins and ends at **Wendover**, a small medieval market town that nestles in a gap in the Chilterns. From Wendover, the walk joins the **Ridgeway**, which climbs up onto **Coombe Hill**, the highest viewpoint in the Chilterns, before looping around the **Chequers Estate**, the prime minister's country retreat. Beyond Chequers, the route heads into the village of **Great Kimble**, where the splendid *Bernard Arms* makes for a good **lunchtime** break. The return route to Wendover takes you along public footpaths through the rich agricultural land of the **Vale of Aylesbury**.

Getting started

0.5km

The walk begins at **Wendover station**, though it's worth making time to look around Wendover town itself before setting off on the walk – the High Street, lined with timber-framed houses, is particularly attractive. To begin the walk, turn right out of the station and head up to the main road; turn right onto this and head out of Wendover via the road bridge over the busy A413 and on past a short row of flint and brick cottages. After a couple of hundred metres you reach a bend in the road; on the opposite side of the road there's a large brown sign for Bacombe Hill by two way-marked tracks. Cross the road and take the right-hand track, waymarked as part of the **Ridgeway** (see p.121; waymarkers show a white acorn on a brown post). A few metres beyond, bear left onto a side track, still following the Ridgeway signs, and head uphill along a steep and muddy path.

Bacombe Hill and Coombe Hill

2km

The path climbs steeply for 300m, then levels off, rising gently along the northern flank of **Bacombe Hill** to reach the summit of **Coombe Hill**, 2km beyond. The track is well signposted, and there are superb views north and west over the Vale of Aylesbury and back across Wendover.

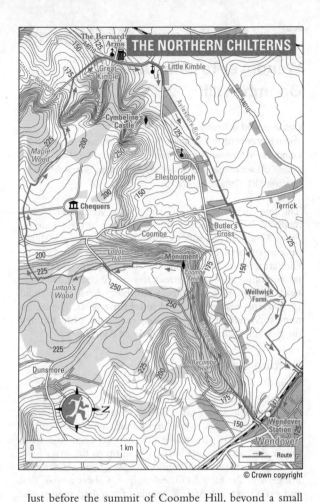

© Crown copyright

Just before the summit of Coombe Hill, beyond a small thicket of trees, you pass through a kissing gate and the view opens up to reveal the **Boer War monument** that tops the hill and dominates the skyline for miles around. Built in 1904 and topped by a gilded sculpture representing an eternal flame, the monument was erected to honour the dead of the Royal Bucks Hussars. The monument stands in a 106-acre National Trust site which was gifted in 1918 by Arthur Hamilton, who also gave the nearby Chequers Estate to the nation (see p.178).

Coombe Hill to Chequers

2.5km

From Coombe Hill, head for the Ridgeway waymarker by the row of trees, just to the left of the monument as you approach it from Wendover. Continue south for a few hundred metres along the western flank of the hill. The hillside falls away steeply to your right down to the hamlet of **Coombe**, while beyond, to the southeast, the Chequers Estate begins to come into view, nestling in the lee of angular Beacon Hill, with the red-brick chimney tops of its Elizabethan manor house poking out from the trees.

The grassy track continues gently downhill for 500m before turning left and rising steeply back up into the trees on the wooded hilltop; a few metres into the woods you reach a kissing gate in the fence to your right. This marks the southern boundary of the National Trust property and takes you along the Chilterns escarpment, here called **Lodge Hill**, for 250m to reach a quiet lane through the woodland opposite a handsome red-brick and flint cottage. Turn right and follow the lane downhill for a few metres to an access road into **Lodge Hill Farm**, set in a small woodland clearing on the opposite side of the road.

Walk down this track for a few metres and then cross the stile in the fence to your right to regain the Ridgeway through **Linton's Wood**. In the woods, carry straight on, heading over a second stile just a few metres beyond the farm access road, and then continue for 300m to reach the first of five waymarked intersections in the woods. These lead after 700m to a wide dirt track; turn right along this to come out of the woods in 400m at a bend in a tarred lane. The kissing gate opposite marks the southeast corner of the Chequers Estate – hence the CCTV cameras that carefully watch over it.

Chequers to Great Kimble

3km

Pass through the kissing gate and into the estate itself – there are superb views from here up to the mid-sixteenth-century manor house of **Chequers**, which has been the country retreat of British prime ministers since the early twentieth century. Lloyd George was the first prime minister to make use of the house, while Winston Churchill often retreated here during the air raids of World War II, and delivered some of his most famous broadcasts from the house. It's regularly used by incumbent prime ministers, both as a retreat from the day-to-day wrangles of political life, and for hosting visiting heads of state (see box opposite).

The house (along with a £100,000 endowment) was given to the nation in 1921 by **Arthur Hamilton** on condition that it be used as the country retreat of the incumbent prime minister. Born in Britain, but half-American, the well-connected and ambitious Hamilton had previously enjoyed a glittering military career, becoming a close friend of Teddy Roosevelt along the way, and later being elected Conservative MP for Fareham and the First Lord of the

Admiralty. In recognition of his services – and possibly a little influenced by his generous donations to the state – the British government elevated him to the status of Viscount Lee of Fareham in 1922.

Records show that there has been a settlement on the site since Roman times, though nothing remains of these early buildings. The current house dates from the mid-sixteenth century and, despite the addition of some Gothic features in the nineteenth century, it retains a largely Elizabethan appearance – all red brick, leaded windows and soaring chimneys. Remember, though, that this is a private estate and stick to the public footpath, which heads west, over the main drive and on to a kissing gate; go through the kissing gate, across the drive just north of the lodge houses, through a second kissing gate and into a field.

The track climbs gently for 400m through the field towards Maple Wood. At the edge of the wood, turn right and follow the track for about 500m to reach another kissing gate – there are superb views from the wood back across the valley

Gins and tonic: Boris Yeltsin at Chequers

During its time as the British prime minister's retreat, Chequers has played host to dignitaries from around the world. Perhaps the most popular anecdote about a VIP visit concerns the then Russian president, **Boris Yeltsin**, who stayed at Chequers in the mid-1990s. After a series of lengthy meetings with the Russian premier, prime minister John Major suggested that they go for a walk to get some fresh air. And so the two world leaders, their wives and a large entourage of diplomats and security officers set out across the Buckinghamshire countryside.

Within a few hundred metres, however, it became apparent that the Russian president was not one of life's great walkers, and he began to look decidedly grumpy as they climbed up to the brow of a hill. At the top, Major presented Yeltsin with three choices: walk back over the fields to Chequers – to which Yeltsin grunted; climb down the hill to the waiting cars and be driven back to the estate – another grunt; or walk on to the old-fashioned English pub, the *Bernard Arms*, in the village of Great Kimble. At this final suggestion, Yeltsin perked up considerably, shouting gleefully, "Gins and tonic! Gins and tonic!" Arriving in Great Kimble, however, they found that the pub was shut. Yeltsin started hammering on the door, yelling, "Open up! This is the president of Russia!" To which the dry reply came from inside: "Oh yes? And I'm the Kaiser." When the pub was finally opened, Major ordered a pint, while Yeltsin asked for a bottle of vodka, only to be refused such a large measure by the nonplussed barmaid. A diplomatic incident was avoided when the Russian president agreed to drink his vodka a glass at a time – like everyone else.

floor to Chequers and beyond to the monument atop Coombe Hill. At the kissing gate, turn left and away from Chequers, heading uphill across a grassy field, over the brow of the hill and down to another kissing gate. Pass through this and head on down the track. After 100m the track opens up onto a wide grassy field, the boundary of the Chequers Estate, marked to your right by a low fence. Take the right-hand public footpath off the Ridgeway and head over to the woods on the far side of the field. Here, a part cobbled-brick and part dirt track heads downhill to a tarred lane and leads after a couple of hundred metres to a T-junction with the A4010. Turn right here and head uphill into **Great Kimble** – little more than a church, a row of Victorian cottages and a pub – the last, the *Bernard Arms*, stands 150m from the lane, just beyond St Nicholas's church, and makes a good spot for **lunch**.

The *Bernard Arms* (℡ 01844/346172) serves excellent lunches from both its set menu and its daily specials board, including a few tasty vegetarian options, plus good seasonal salads, soups and stews.

Great Kimble to Ellesborough: the Aylesbury Ring

2.5km

From the pub, continue north along the A4010. After 500m, turn right down **Ellesborough Road**, following the black signs for a few hundred metres to reach the **Aylesbury Ring**, a 52-kilometre circular trail which leads through some of the valley's most rural landscapes, sticking mainly to farmland tracks and passing through small villages – the return walk to Wendover lies along it. Continue for 500m, through **Little Kimble**, passing the village church, **All Saints**, which boasts some of the finest Jacobean wall paintings in the county, featuring numerous saints, including St Francis preaching to the birds and the martyrdom of St Margaret. The most striking of the panels is that on the west wall, showing two fallen women being pushed into hell by the devil himself. Continue past the church straight on towards Ellesborough; ignore the green public footpath sign to the left just beyond the church.

About 500m beyond the turn-off from the A4010, on the edge of Little Kimble and, confusingly, at the village limit sign for Ellesborough (though this village lies a further 1km up the road), turn left and cross the stile next to a modern house, following another black sign (it's a little lost in the house's hedge), to the Aylesbury Ring – this is still a dedicated public footpath, although you might feel as if you're trespassing since the footpath has been incorporated into the house's lawn. After a few metres, the footpath bends round to the right, continuing between the older properties at the edge of Little Kimble.

After 100m, at the end of this short track between the houses, cross over a stile and out into farmland, and continue straight on. Almost immediately, Ellesborough's church comes into view, an impressive Victorian flint and brick pile with an imposing stair-turret tower, sitting proudly on a small hill at the roadside a few hundred metres off to your right. To the right of the church rises the man-made mound nicknamed **Cymbeline's Mount** – the motte of a small medieval castle.

Ellesborough to Wellwick Farm

2.5km

The track here leads across the rich arable farmland of the **Vale of Aylesbury**; to your right, the Chiltern escarpment rises steeply above the villages – Little Kimble, Ellesborough and Butler's Cross – strung out along the Ellesborough Road, itself a good 500m beyond and above the public footpath. Follow the public footpath, passing below the church and crossing three stiles to come out after 800m at the end of a lane by the thatched Springs Cottage. Head straight on along the lane, which marks the southern boundary of Ellesborough; where it bends round to go up to the main road, pick up the trail at a stile to the left of the houses and head on, over a second stile and between two fields. Crossing over three more stiles, the path passes through fields and paddocks to come out after around 500m at the busy road into Butler's Cross.

Turn left, cross the road just beyond some houses and pick up the path on the far side at yet another stile. The track continues east, passing over two more stiles and through a gate before climbing gently for 500m to the brow of a hill, then gently downhill again, over three more stiles towards a small copse a further 700m further on. The copse hides the splendid Elizabethan red-brick and flint **Wellwick Farm** from view until you're almost at the house. There are good views of the house as you follow the path, close by its northern facade and on around the easterly side to a stile into a field. From here, follow the waymarkers (here attached to the telegraph poles) up into the farmyard, crossing a couple more stiles en route.

Wellwick Farm to Wendover station

2km

Head out of the farmyard, straight over the access road and into the next field, then follow the waymarkers down the left-hand edge of the field. Just before the hedgerow begins, turn left, passing over the stile and heading straight on towards the bridge – a farmyard track over the A413 – a few hundred metres further on. Cross three more stiles on the track, after which you'll come out in a field just before the bridge. There's a public footpath straight to the bridge, though this is not always respected by the farmer who owns this land, and you may well find it ploughed and muddy in winter and difficult to pass when planted in summer. If so, head round the edge of the field to get to the bridge.

On the far side of the bridge, turn right at the public footpath sign and follow the narrow track, which leads behind houses to emerge on a quiet access road after 200m; this leads to the small industrial estate next to the station. **Wendover station** is just under 500m along this road from here.

Ivinghoe Beacon

Tring to Aldbury

Distance and difficulty: 12.5km; moderate.
Train: Euston to Tring (Mon–Sat every 30min, Sun hourly; 40min);
return from Tring to Euston (Mon–Sat every 30min, Sun hourly;
40min).
Map: OS Landranger 165: *Aylesbury & Leighton Buzzard*; OS
Explorer 181: *Chiltern Hills North*.

This superb circular walk leads from **Tring station** in
Hertfordshire and up onto the Chilterns escarpment. The
first half of the route follows the **Ridgeway Long-Distance
Footpath**, a 136-kilometre hilltop track that begins in
Wiltshire and ends at **Ivinghoe Beacon**, one of the highest
points in the Chiltern Hills (for more on the Ridgeway, see
p.121). Passing through beech woodland and over chalk
uplands, the walk gives fine views over the Vale of Aylesbury,
a patchwork of farmland dotted with small villages and
towns. From Ivinghoe Beacon, the route leads back through
the woods of the extensive **Ashridge Estate**, once the seat
of the dukes of Bridgewater and now home to a network of
public footpaths and some handily placed **tearooms**. Beyond
the **Bridgewater Monument**, which dominates the hillside
hereabouts, the route drops down into the handsome village
of **Aldbury**, with half-timbered cottages and a duck pond.
From Aldbury, it's a short walk back to Tring station.

There's a great **pub**, *The Greyhound Inn*, in Aldbury, but
unfortunately it's located close to the end of the walk. It's
better to take a **picnic** – there are lots of good picnic spots,
not least Ivinghoe Beacon itself – or eat at the National Trust
tearooms by the Bridgewater Monument.

Getting started

0.5km

From **Tring station**, turn right onto Station Road and walk
along it for roughly 400m, passing a turning off to your left.
At a bend in the road, turn left, following the fingerpost sign
for the Ridgeway up the access road to **Westland Farm**.
This short concrete road leads in less than 100m past the
entrance to the farm to a metal gate in the hedgerow, where
you reach the **Ridgeway Long-Distance Footpath**.

Through Aldbury Nowers

1.5km

Turn left onto the Ridgeway and follow it gently uphill
through an avenue of hawthorns behind Westland Farm. After

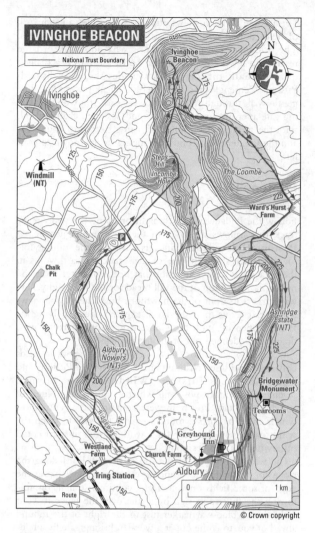

IVINGHOE BEACON

National Trust Boundary

Ivinghoe
Beacon

Ivinghoe

N

Windmill
(NT)

Steps
Hill
Incombe
Hole

The Coombe

Ward's Hurst
Farm

P

Chalk
Pit

Ashridge
Estate
(NT)

Aldbury
Nowers
(NT)

Bridgewater
Monument

Tearooms

Ridgeway

Greyhound
Inn

Westland
Farm

Church Farm

Tring Station

Aldbury

0   1 km

Route

© Crown copyright

600m you come to an intersection with another public footpath; turn right, following the fingerpost signs for the
Ridgeway along the steep track up into **Aldbury Nowers**, a
mature beech wood on the chalky upland above Tring. A few
metres into the wood, turn left off the main track at the next
Ridgeway fingerpost and head up a series of dirt steps. At the
top of the steps, the path veers off to the left (ignore the track
straight ahead) and briefly heads out of the trees, giving great
views across the rich farmland of the **Vale of Aylesbury**.
Within a few metres you begin to climb quite steeply into the
woods again. At the top of this rise, the track, which is clear
and wide at this point, bears right and heads through the heart
of the woodland along the edge of the Chiltern escarpment.

From here there are views out across the valley, a patchwork of fields dotted with small settlements and farm buildings. The dominant feature, however, is what looks like a large reservoir a few kilometres to the northeast. This is actually a disused **chalk pit**, beyond which lies the (also disused) Pitstone Cement Works, for which the chalk pit was dug. The gentle walk through Aldbury Nowers ends at a wooden kissing gate after just under 1km; beyond lies open chalk upland, with the summit of Pitstone Hill rising steeply to your right and the Chilterns escarpment dropping steeply down to your left.

Pitstone Hill

1.5km

Follow the Ridgeway signs straight on along the wide grassy track that follows the edge of the escarpment, just below **Pitstone Hill**, and then winds its way up to the summit, following **Grim's Ditch**, one of many ancient earthworks in the area whose exact function has been forgotten over the millennia. At the top of the hill (head for the blue and yellow waymarkers in front of the hawthorn bush ahead), the views to the east across the Ashridge Estate and ahead to Ivinghoe Beacon open up, with the Chilterns escarpment rising with dramatic suddenness out of the flat farmland.

A couple of kilometres away in the valley below, in fields between the disused chalk pit and the villages of Pitstone and Ivinghoe, stands **Pitstone Windmill**, a traditional, seventeenth-century post mill which is one of the oldest of its type in Britain. Post mills were built around a central post which could be turned round to allow the sails to catch the wind – an essential feature for a working mill in what could otherwise be a windless spot.

The wide grassy path at the top of the hill leads along the ridge for 800m before dropping down steeply, flanking the edge of some fields on your right; continue straight on, following the fingerpost sign by a stile over the fence to your right then a blue waymarker just to the right of the mound ahead of you, to come out at a wooden kissing gate by a telegraph pole.

Incombe Hole and Steps Hill

1.7km

The gate leads through to a picnic area at the edge of a gravel car park. A few metres beyond the picnic area a lane heads left to right towards Pitstone and Ivinghoe villages. Cross the lane and turn left to follow it up to the Ridgeway fingerpost sign a few metres further on at a metal kissing gate opposite the entrance to the car park. Go through this and continue straight on along the wide track through farmland and ahead to the Chiltern escarpment. The bowl of Incombe Hole (see below) lies straight ahead; beyond it, along the rippling folds of the escarpment are, in turn, Steps Hill and Ivinghoe Beacon.

This glacial valley is at its most dramatic here: to either side flat farmland stretches out along the valley floor; ahead, the escarpment rises steeply, the Ridgeway heading straight on and up the escarpment by **Incombe Hole**. A dramatic depression in the escarpment, the "hole" is a good example of a so-called "dry valley", a topographical feature typical of a glacial valley, which was formed by ice melt in the frozen limestone of the escarpment at the end of the last ice age. Follow the track up the escarpment and round the edge of Incombe Hole to a gate and stile 700m or so from the valley bottom (ignore the yellow waymarker off to the right at the bend).

Following the waymarkers, continue along a track to the left of the gate and stile and head into the hawthorn thicket ahead; the way through the thicket is clear and well marked, and brings you out after around 100m to the grassy side of **Steps Hill**. Head downhill for a further hundred metres, keeping close to the barbed-wire fence to your right and go out of the field through the kissing gate. This leads up to the right and over scrubland for 300m before heading downhill to a bend in a road (Beacon Road) that runs round the base of Ivinghoe Beacon.

Ivinghoe Beacon

1km

Cross the road, on the far side of which you'll find the junction of three waymarked public footpaths. Go left here and up the final 500-metre ascent to the top of **Ivinghoe Beacon**. The last few metres are a steep scramble, but worth it for the panoramic views: south and west across the Chilterns and the Vale of Aylesbury respectively, north towards Buckingham and the Midlands, and east along Gallows Hill towards Whipsnade and the Dunstable Downs.

Ivinghoe Beacon marks the northern end of the Ridgeway Long-Distance Footpath, though the ancient trail is thought to have once continued down off the escarpment and on towards East Anglia. Standing 223m high, the hill takes its name from the beacons that were periodically lit here, part of an early warning system against potential invasion from Roman times through the Spanish Armada to World War II. Ivinghoe Beacon was also the site of one of Britain's earliest **hillforts**; metalwork and pottery finds from its summit indicate that it was occupied from as early as the eighth or seventh century BC, and you can still make out parts of the enclosure and fortifications – including the ditches and mounds that bounded the fort – at the summit.

Through The Coombe

2.3km

From the beacon, retrace your steps back down to the three waymarked public footpaths by Beacon Road and go right. After 100m this path leads to a stile at the edge of sheep-farming land. You're now on the **Icknield Way**, another famous long-distance footpath, which you follow for the next couple of kilometres. Cross over the stile and head down across the field to a gate 150m further on; go through the gate and continue straight on.

After 400m you reach another stile, leading into the field to your right. Cross this and take the lower of two paths that lead away from the stile and around the side of the hill before you – a few metres from the stile you'll spot a yellow waymarker in the distance pointing towards a beech wood. This is **The Coombe**, an outlying part of the Ashridge Estate (see below). The track through it is easy to follow for the first 600m, after which you come to the edge of a well-established fir plantation, with rows of giant firs stretching on ahead of you. The track, marked by a yellow waymarker at this point, is just to the left of the row of firs directly in front of you. Follow the path as it zigzags between the rows of trees to emerge after 300m at the edge of the woodland.

Follow the yellow waymarker at this point heading straight on along the edge of the woods and then up the steep, wooded bank that rises a few metres ahead of you. The initial sharp climb is followed by a long, steady ascent to a stile at the far (southerly) end of The Coombe, just before **Ward's Hurst Farm**. Cross the stile and continue along the edge of the field beyond it to come out into the farmyard by a fingerpost. The route leaves the Icknield Way at this point; turn right, following the public footpath signs, and go through the farmyard and down the drive back to **Beacon Road**.

The Bridgewater Monument

1km

Cross Beacon Road and head into the beech woods at the public footpath sign opposite. The path heads into the heart of the National Trust-managed **Ashridge Estate**, the former estate of the dukes of Bridgewater. A few metres on from Beacon Road, turn right onto a wide dirt track and follow this round for 300m in a long, gradual curve as it heads down through the woodland to a crossroads. Turn left here (ignoring the yellow waymarkers straight on down a minor track), following the main track along the chalky ridge through the heart of the estate; you'll soon start to see official waymarkers for the **Ashridge Estate Boundary Trail** every few hundred metres.

The trail follows a ridge of the Chilterns for 2km, giving good views out across the valley towards Aldbury Nowers, passing a bijou log cabin and crossing a wooden bridge over a dry ditch (part of an ancient earthworks) before coming out at the **Bridgewater Monument**. The monument is also owned by the National Trust; you can climb to the top (April–Oct Sat & Sun noon–5pm; £1.20) for great views out across the surrounding countryside. The monument – a Doric column topped by a square plinth and copper bowl – was erected in 1837 in honour of Francis, third duke of Bridgewater, the "father of inland navigation". The duke, inspired by the navigational waterways he'd seen in France, commissioned the building of a canal at his coal mine in Worsley, northwest of Manchester, in the late 1760s. Though not the country's first canal (the Sankey Brook Navigation Canal in St Helen's claims that title), the **Bridgewater Canal**, as it became known, was the prototype for the man-made waterways that crisscrossed the country by the early nineteenth century.

The National Trust tearooms in front of the monument (Tues–Sun noon–4 or 5pm, also Mon in summer), serve soups, sandwiches and jacket potatoes, as well as afternoon teas.

Aldbury to Tring station

3km

Head straight across the clearing and follow the track beyond the car park outside the tearooms, waymarked as part of the **Hertfordshire Way**, a 265-kilometre, circular long-distance footpath round the county. The path leads downhill, ever more steeply, through a cutting in the chalky hillside to come out after just under 1km in the village of **Aldbury**. Turn right along the lane and head down to the handsome village green, complete with a reed-lined duck pond and village stocks, and surrounded by half-timbered Tudor cottages, a tiny village post office, a medieval church and the welcoming *Greyhound Inn*.

The Greyhound Inn (☏ 01442/851278) serves lunches daily.

To return to Tring station, head straight along Station Road past the church. Just beyond the churchyard, and before a bend in the road, turn right and head through a kissing gate (it's rather buried in the hedgerow). The path heads over another stile and across a paddock behind the farm buildings of **Church Farm**. A few metres ahead you'll see another kissing gate, by the line of buildings to your left. Go through this and turn right, exiting the paddock onto a dirt track that runs behind the farmyard buildings and beside a hedgerow to reach two metal gates, either side of a farm track; go through these and carry straight on between fields to a wooden kissing gate, some 750m beyond the farm. Here, the path meets a bridleway, just before a golf course; turn left onto the bridleway and follow it downhill for 600m to a metal gate and down some steps to return to the **Ridgeway**, just by Westland Farm.

From here, retrace your steps: go straight on, through the metal gate on the opposite side of the Ridgeway track and down the concrete road, past the gate into **Westland Farm**, to the lane (Station Road). Turn right and follow this lane back to **Tring station**, a few hundred metres further on.

Around Blenheim Palace

Long Hanborough to Blenheim Palace and North Leigh Roman Villa

Distance and difficulty: 11km, plus 7km detour; moderate.
Trains: London Paddington to Hanborough (Mon–Sat hourly, Sun every 2hr; 1hr 15min); return from Hanborough to London Paddington (Mon–Sat hourly, Sun every 2hr; 1hr 15min).
Map: OS Landranger 164: *Oxford*; OS Explorer 180: *Oxford*.

This walk runs from the Oxfordshire village of **Bladon**, where Winston Churchill is buried, to his birthplace, the Baroque masterpiece **Blenheim Palace**. The route initially skirts the park and runs to the genteel and fantastically pretty small town of **Woodstock**. The pub food on offer there isn't great – if you want **lunch** it's better to buy a picnic at the excellent deli in Woodstock or head for the café in the palace grounds.

Beyond the palace, the route curves through open parkland designed by Capability Brown. Having left the palace grounds, you can either return via country lanes to the station at Long Hanborough, or make a circular **detour** across glorious country to the modest Romano-British remains of **North Leigh Roman Villa** (you're unlikely to have time to make the detour if you do the Blenheim Palace tour, unless you get an early start).

To Woodstock

4km

From Hanborough **station**, turn right onto the busy A4095. Though you'll see entrances to the park on your left, these are either restricted to local residents or private, so you need to stick to the main road. After 1.5km you come to the village of **Bladon**; the churchyard where **Winston Churchill** is buried is to the right, up a flight of steps. The surprisingly simple grave lies just beyond the entrance to the church.

Some 750m beyond Bladon you come to a small, triangular green on the left with a road leading up to a gatehouse. To the right of this road, under a big horse chestnut tree, is a **footpath** sign; follow this across a stile, then go up the faint grassy path which skirts the park – the park wall lies to the left. Continue across the field until you come to some farm buildings on the left, then cross the stile ahead to reach the

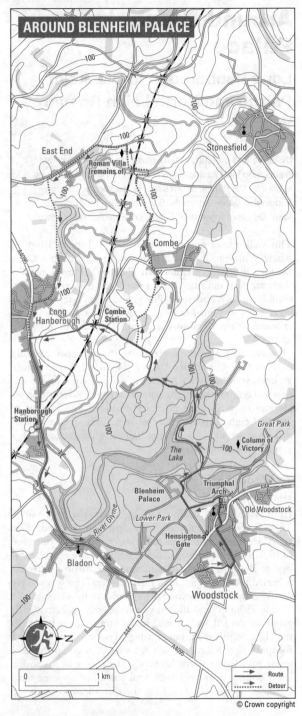

AROUND BLENHEIM PALACE

East End

Roman Villa (remains of)

Stonesfield

Combe

Long Hanborough

Combe Station

Hanborough Station

Great Park

Column of Victory

The Lake

Blenheim Palace

Triumphal Arch

Old Woodstock

Lower Park

River Glyme

Hensington Gate

Bladon

Woodstock

| | Route |
| | Detour |

© Crown copyright

A44. To go straight to the park, bypassing Woodstock, turn left along the A44 for 700m, then take a left to reach **Hensington Gate** (daily 9am to dusk; £2.50, or free with palace ticket), then continue to the bridge in front of the palace (see below) to pick up the continuation of the walk. Alternatively, to go **into Woodstock**, cross the A44 and follow the footpath straight ahead of you, signed for Hensington. The path edges the fields for 400m, then joins a suburban street. Turn right into The Covert and go straight ahead, down Willoughby Way, following the footpath sign. Where the footpath emerges, turn left and, after 100m, take another left, following New Road and the signs for the town centre.

After 500m you come out onto the main road through Woodstock, with the *Punchbowl Inn* on your left. Turn right and cross the road for *Zakis Deli*. To continue to the palace grounds, go past the deli and take the first left onto Market Street. Head past the *Bear Hotel* and, at the road's end, you reach the **Triumphal Arch**, the dramatic entry point for the park.

....

Zakis Deli at 31–33 Oxford St in Woodstock is a great
place to buy a picnic, with organic bread, local cheeses,
meats and good bottled beer for sale. Another option for
lunch is the café in the palace grounds.

....

Blenheim Palace grounds

4.5km

The Triumphal Arch leads into the **palace grounds** (9am to dusk; £2.50, or free with palace ticket). Follow the curving path to the left to reach the palace itself (see opposite), then cross Vanbrugh's **bridge** – which was conceived to resemble a Roman aqueduct – over the vast artificial lake designed by Capability Brown. In an echo of the victorious note sounded by the palace itself, Capability planted the park's trees so that they represented the formation of the battalions of soldiers at the Battle of Blenheim. The view is dominated by a **statue** of the first Duke of Marlborough, who poses fetchingly in a toga atop the tall Column of Victory.

Some 100m beyond the bridge, go through the wooden gate to the left and follow the path, which now runs through woodland, skirting the lake, for 1.5km, until you come out at a T-junction under a stand of tall copper beeches – this is at the point where the lake peters out. Turn left along the track and soon after go left through a gate and then follow the grassy path which runs uphill, curving past some fir trees. You then join a tarred path; turn left onto that and carry on up the hill. Finally, on the right, there's a turning to **Combe Gate**; you'll see the gatehouse through the trees.

Blenheim Palace

> Altho' the building was to be calculated for and adapted to a private habitation, yet it ought at the same time, to be considered both as a Royall and a National Monument and care taken in the design, and the execution, that it might have the qualitys proper to such a monument, vitz, Beauty, Magnificence and Duration.
>
> John Vanbrugh, architect of Blenheim Palace

When John Churchill, first Duke of Marlborough, defeated the French at the Battle of Blenheim on the Danube in 1704, his reward from a grateful nation was the royal estate at Woodstock, and a staggering £240,000 (worth £25 million today) with which to build a suitable home.

The result was the remarkable **Blenheim Palace**, built by John Vanbrugh assisted by Nicholas Hawksmoor. The palace was conceived in a spirit of celebration and triumph, and the humiliation of the French and their king is trumpeted by many subtle and not-so-subtle devices. The gateways to the stable courtyards feature carvings depicting the Lion of England attacking the Cock of France; a bust of Louis XIV was stuck on the south front of Blenheim, "like a head on a stake", as the duke described it; while in the palace rooms a portrait of the French king is flanked by tapestries depicting the battle, with English soldiers charging towards their victim from either side.

The triumphalism is tempered by a strong theatrical element, evident in the arcaded lines of the building, and in the stage-like central courtyard, a strangely blank space which seems to be awaiting some drama – this quality may stem from the fact that Vanbrugh was also a well-known playwright. Certain features of the building are whimsical and high-spirited, notably the fanciful pinnacles and turrets that run along the rooftop and lighten the sculptural symmetry of the palace.

Blenheim Palace is open mid-March to Oct daily 10.30–5.30pm; £10 for an excellent if rather brisk 45min tour; Ⓦwww.blenheimpalace.com. The price includes admission to the Churchill exhibition and access to the palace courtyard, Pleasure Gardens, Herb Garden and Butterfly House. The house is still in private hands, and access to the family rooms in the east wing is at the eleventh Duke's discretion.

Vanbrugh's genius went unappreciated in his time. The Duchess of Marlborough would have preferred Christopher Wren, but the duke – who had been impressed by Vanbrugh's designs for Castle Howard – overruled her. The duchess was openly hostile to Vanbrugh, and it was left to Hawksmoor to act as diplomat. Money ran short, the duchess accused Vanburgh of mismanagement and he finally left, deeply offended, taking Hawksmoor with him. The building was then completed under the direction of the duchess, who watered down many of the original designs, which were by general consensus considered overly flamboyant and even vulgar. When Vanbrugh tried to visit the palace in 1725, a year before his death, he was refused entry.

If you **tour** the palace, you may feel just a little sympathy for the duchess, who had wanted "a clean sweet house and garden be it ever so small". The scale of the interior is emphatically undomestic; the palace is built entirely on one floor, with hugely high ceilings (three of them sculpted in stucco and gold leaf by Hawksmoor). The rooms were originally conceived to run into each other, providing sweeping vistas that, however visually dramatic, must have been a little overwhelming to actually live in. Subsequent restructuring – some carried out during World War II when the palace was the home of MI5 – has closed off several corridors.

Blenheim to Long Hanborough

3km

Turn right out of Combe Gate onto the narrow country lane, and then left at the junction, following the sign to Long Hanborough. This road leads down to Combe station; if you want to take the **detour** to North Leigh Roman Villa (see below), turn right into the meadow after 250m, following the green footpath sign to Combe.

Missing out the detour, carry on down the road to **Combe station**. You may be able to get a train from here back to London, but the service is limited. To get to Hanborough station, follow the road under the railway line and continue for 200m, crossing the bridge across the River Evenlode. Just over the bridge, follow the footpath sign which points directly ahead of you (don't turn left onto the track here, as the route has become overgrown). The path leads across a field for 500m, eventually emerging at the A4095. Turn left, and follow the road for 1.5km to **Hanborough station**.

Detour to North Leigh Roman Villa

7km

The detour to **North Leigh Roman Villa** makes a moderately strenuous but enjoyable cross-country circuit. Though the remains of the villa aren't exactly breathtaking, it's fun to discover them as you tramp across a field, and the church at **Combe** with its medieval wall paintings is well worth a look.

Across country to Combe

1km

The **public footpath** leading off the road to Combe station runs for 250m to a clump of woodland – skirt the woodland, keeping it to your right, then turn right into the field, following the yellow arrow, and take the path across the field. This is a gorgeous part of the walk, with a thatched cottage to the right and the tower of Combe church ahead.

The path leads straight across two fields towards the church and comes out at the village playing field, just opposite **St Laurence's Church**. This is a handsome fourteenth-century parish church whose unusually wide nave is decorated with vivid fifteenth-century **wall paintings**. These were painted over following the Reformation, and uncovered in 1892. Though the figures are painted rather crudely, with heavy outlines, the scenes are lively and inventive and the scheme as a whole must have been strikingly colourful. The most substantial tableau is over the chancel arch, and would have sent an unequivocal message to the medieval congregation. It depicts the Last Judgement, with Christ seated on a rainbow, the blessed floating up serenely from their graves to his right and, to his left, the damned being poked down into the open mouth of hell by red demons. Other paintings show the Crucifixion, set in a border of stylized clouds, to the left of the chancel arch; a much damaged St Christopher, on the south wall, with a shark, an otter, fish and a mermaid frolicking in the river around him; and, to the right of the chancel arch, the touching fragments of an Annunciation scene, with just the eyes and wing-tip of the Angel remaining, and the hand of God floating above. Apart from the paintings, look out for the medieval **stained glass** and the **pulpit**, decorated with blind tracery.

Combe to North Leigh Roman Villa

2km

Coming out of the church, turn left into **Combe** to reach the village green and pub; turn left along the green and follow the road signposted to Long Hanborough. Turn right immediately after the renovated chapel and carry on up the road, continuing straight ahead, past Chatterpie Lane.

From here, continue straight on for 750m, past the sewage works, to **Lower Westfield Farm**. Go through the gate just beyond the farm buildings; the track leads across and down the field – turn right along the stream through the gate and then take a left over the bridge that leads across the stream. Turn left immediately, with the stream on your left, and carry on till you pass under the railway bridge. Just beyond the bridge, head across the field to the right; you can see the buildings of North Leigh Roman Villa from here. Cross a stile to go along the field, with the villa to your left; go through the hedge to reach the villa ruins.

North Leigh Roman Villa

North Leigh Roman Villa is one of many such remains which dot the area, its extent marked by low foundation walls. A modern structure has been built to protect the partially intact **mosaic floor**; the door is generally locked, but you can see the floor through a large viewing window.

The very term "Roman villa" is rather misleading; by the fourth century, when this villa's buildings reached their most developed form, such houses would have been built and lived in by Britons. Although these villas featured Roman-style courtyards and bathhouses, they were otherwise so adapted to a colder climate that they resembled later manor houses rather than continental Roman villas. Like a manor house, this villa was essentially a farm, whose inhabitants were self-supporting, except for luxury items such as the mosaic floor itself. This, rather prosaically, would have been ordered from one of seven factories in Cirencester – buyers chose a design from plans issued by the factory, and the floor would have been constructed there, rather than in situ at the villa. Slabs of mosaic floor were wrapped in straw and transported to the site by bullock cart, and the slabs were then laid, the skill being to disguise the joins between them. The interlocking geometric decoration that edges the floor was for good luck, a charm protecting anyone who stood within it.

To Long Hanborough via East End

4km

From the villa, take the main track up the hill and turn left, heading up to a minor road, where you turn left. The road leads through the pretty, straggling village of **East End**. Walk right through the village, ignoring the first footpath sign on the left-hand side, then turn left at the second path, 100m further on, marked with a blue bridleway sign. The path runs for around 750m, dipping down the field and then up past woodland before joining the minor road into Long Hanborough; carry on straight ahead for 750m. You come to a junction with a pub on the left-hand side – go straight ahead here till the road joins the A4095. Turn left, and follow the road for 1.5km – **Hanborough station** is on the right.

8

St Albans to Bedfordshire

The affluent and densely populated county of **Hertfordshire** provides the setting for the first two walks in this chapter, both set on or near the course of **Watling Street**, the great Roman Road that once ran from Londinium (London) to Deva (Chester), and both liberally dotted with the remains of previous eras, from Roman villas to Belgic earthworks. The first walk leads from the medieval market town of **St Albans**, through Roman Verulamium, to the manor houses of the Gorhambury Estate. The second begins and ends in **Harpenden**, a stop north of St Albans on the railway line from London, following the Lea Valley Way to nearby Wheathampstead, on whose eastern limits are the massive earthworks of Oppidum. Further north is Bedfordshire's chief attraction, the **Woburn Estate**, with an impressive stately home and England's largest safari park.

St Albans and Harpenden are both connected to **King's Cross Thameslink** by fast and frequent **train** services. The walk to Woburn begins on a branch line between Bletchley (services from Euston) and Bedford (King's Cross Thameslink). Most King's Cross Thameslink services call at West Hampstead, while those from Euston usually call at Harrow & Wealdstone. Tickets are surprisingly good value for all routes.

The St Albans and Wheathampstead walks are both close to London, so good if you don't fancy an early start. The Woburn Abbey walk will take the best part of a day, especially if you plan to visit the abbey itself or make the additional loop around the park, so aim to start walking by no later than around 11am. All the walks in this chapter follow a circular route, meaning that they're convenient if you're **driving**.

The Lea Valley Way

Harpenden via Wheathampstead to Oppidum

Distance and difficulty: 15.5km; moderate.
Train: King's Cross Thameslink to Harpenden (every 5–10min; 30–45min); Harpenden to King's Cross Thameslink (every 5–10min; 30–45min).
Map: OS Landranger 166: *Luton & Hertford*; OS Explorer 182: *St Albans & Hatfield*.

This varied walk starts from the pleasant commuter town of **Harpenden** and heads along the **Lea Valley Way** – an 80-kilometre walk that follows the **River Lea** (or Lee, as it's sometimes spelt) from its source north of Luton to the River Thames. The route passes through the handsome medieval village of **Wheathampstead**, named for the wheat that was harvested and milled there for over a millennium. Beyond Wheathampstead the walk heads through the massive earthworks, known as the **Devil's Dyke**, which once protected the Celtic settlement of **Oppidum**, then continues southwest into **Nomansland Common** and on to nearby **Amwell**, where the *Elephant & Castle* pub makes a great stop for **lunch**, though it doesn't open on Sundays; a good alternative is the *Wicked Lady*, just outside Wheathampstead. From Amwell, the route continues north to rejoin the Lea Valley Way and head back into Harpenden.

Getting started

2km

Turn right out of Harpenden **train station** and head down the station drive to the main road; turn right here, go through the tunnel under the railway and uphill along Station Road (the B652). Continue along this busy thoroughfare for just over 1km to reach the **River Lea** at a bend in the road, with grassy slopes running down to the river at a series of weirs, a popular spot with the feel of a village green. Take the path down the right-hand side of a hawthorn hedge, which leads down from the bend in the road to the river, then turn right, following the **Lea Valley Way** signs along the near side of the river, passing the weirs by a children's playground and following the dirt track along the river-bank.

After 300m you come out at a lane. Turn right here and continue 100m to reach a left-hand turn into a lane by the *Marquis of Granby* pub. Houses line the right-hand side of the lane; to the left, fields lead down to the river. After just over

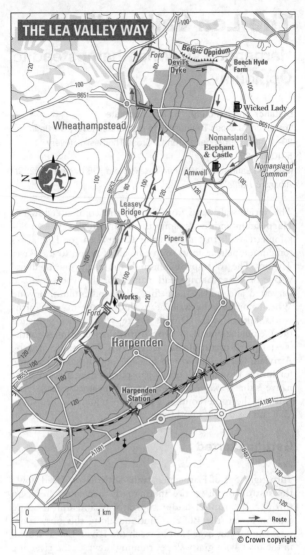

© Crown copyright

200m you pass under a bridge at the entrance to a small sewage works (don't worry: things will improve shortly). Take the steps on your left up onto the track over the lane, then turn right, following the **Lea Valley Way** signs, which lead you quickly out of town and into open countryside.

Into Wheathampstead

3km

The well-maintained track continues east out of Harpenden, with views across the shallow **Lea Valley**, the river meandering below you along the valley floor. To your right, Piggotshill Wood stands on the hillside, while below it the greens of a golf course run down to the public footpath. A kilometre or so from Harpenden, you reach the hamlet of **Leasey Bridge**. Turn right and walk 50m along the lane to **Little Croft**, a modern bungalow looking a little out of place amongst the Victorian cottages; the public footpath, clearly waymarked from the verge of the lane, leads right up the bungalow's driveway to a metal kissing gate in the hedgerow to the right. Go through this to come out into a paddock behind the housing, then head diagonally across the field to reach a second kissing gate in the far corner. Keeping the hedgerow close to your right, continue uphill to reach a third kissing gate 100m further on, just to the right of a large barn. Remember this point for later on, since you'll return here towards the end of the walk.

Go through the gate and turn left onto the track in front of the barn, following the Lea Valley Way signs along a dirt track that leads left then right, at first following the boundaries of the neighbouring paddocks for 250m, then heading along a hawthorn hedge out into farmed land. The path is some 20m above the valley floor at this point, giving good views over the surrounding countryside and scattered farm buildings, and over to Gustard Wood, which stands on the hillside on the far side of the valley. Some 600m further on, go through the wooden kissing gate in the hedgerow ahead and straight on across the field on the opposite side towards the modern development that marks the western edge of Wheathampstead.

Wheathampstead

0.5km

The attractive medieval town of **Wheathampstead** developed – and was named – as a result of local wheat production, for which this part of Hertfordshire was well known prior to the Industrial Revolution; there was a working mill on the river here since at least 1086. It's now a popular commuter town, as demonstrated by the rash of modern housing developments which mar its outskirts, though the old high street preserves an attractive clutch of half-timbered and brick cottages.

The public footpath along the Lea Valley leads into town through a functional 1970s housing estate, running behind it for 200m before leading via a short alley into the estate itself. At the end of the alley, turn left and head down to a T-junction (there are generic yellow waymarkers on the telegraph poles), then turn right and follow the waymarkers (still on the telegraph poles) for 100m to reach the main **Harpenden Road**. Turn left here for a dozen metres to reach a T-junction with Wheathampstead's High Street. Just to your left is the village church, **St Helen's**, on Bury Green. Built in the late fourteenth century, the flint church is topped by an unusual lead-clad broach spire, which begins like a pyramidal roof and culminates in an octagonal spire – a Victorian addition, built in imitation of an earlier medieval one.

Turn left onto the High Street, a particularly attractive spot, lined with whitewashed medieval cottages, and head downhill for 200m to return to the banks of the River Lea. Straddling the river is **Wheathampstead Mill**, a brick structure dating from the sixteenth century which continued in operation until the early twentieth century; it's now home to a small butcher's.

Towards Devil's Dyke

1.5km

Cross the river and take the first turning right into another modern housing estate at the edge of the village. Follow the waymarkers, which take you out of the estate after 100m and over a rough track, leading straight on past an area of bulrushes to emerge in open countryside – keep to the main wide track, ignoring the public footpath that forks off to the right just beyond the bulrushes. For the next kilometre the track runs a few metres above the riverbank before ending at a wooden kissing gate by the **Cory-Wright Way**, Wheathampstead's bypass road.

Go through the gate, turn right and head down the dirt track parallel to the road. After 150m you reach a wider track. Turn right and follow this track down to the river and over the ford just before **Marford Farm** (there's a footbridge to the right of the ford, useful if the river is in spate and you don't want to get your feet wet). Here, the track becomes a lane. Follow it for 300m up to a main road, then cross the road and carry straight on, up Dyke Lane, following waymarkers for the **Hertfordshire Way**, a long-distance footpath that makes a 265-kilometre circuit of the county.

Devil's Dyke to Amwell

3km

Just 200m from the main road, a high, wrought-iron gate, flanked by red-brick gateposts, marks the northern end of **Devil's Dyke**. This is the western defensive ditch of **Oppidum**, the earliest capital of the Belgic Catuvellauni tribe. The 100-acre site, now farmland, was first excavated in the 1930s, and again in the 1970s; all the finds are now on display at the Verulamium Museum in St Albans (see p.209). Go through the gates and walk through the dyke itself, whose massive fortifications are still an impressive site: a tree-filled dell up to twelve metres deep, forty metres wide and half a kilometre long. The dyke is one of two remaining earthworks bounding the site; the second, **The Slad**, lies 600m to the east – it's just as impressive, but unfortunately lies on private land.

At the far end of Devil's Dyke, you come out at the edge of some fields. Bear right and head across to the hedgerow beyond the line of trees at the edge of the field to reach a gap back out onto Dyke Lane. Turn left along the lane and continue for 300m to the public footpath signs opposite the entrance to **Beech Hyde Farm**. Turn right, taking the track across open fields back towards Wheathampstead. Some 300m from the lane, the track runs behind houses to come out after 200m at the main road into the village from the south.

Go straight across this and turn left, following public footpath signs downhill towards **Nomansland Common**, which you reach after 800m, emerging opposite the *Wicked Lady* pub, a good alternative to the *Elephant & Castle* for **lunch**. The common's unusual name derives from an ecclesiastical squabble in the fifteenth century, when the monasteries of St Albans and Westminster both claimed it as part of their territory. After twenty years of wrangling, a jury ordered that both parishes should share it as grazing land – hence the moniker of No Man's Land, which the common retains to this day.

The restaurant at the *Wicked Lady* (☎01582/832128) serves hearty lunches and evening meals – honey roast lamb, steak and mushroom pie – daily from noon to 10pm.

Opposite the *Wicked Lady* pub, a small access road leads off to your right to some cricket huts. Cross straight over this and onto the edge of the cricket pitch, following the line of benches straight on. At the third bench, bear right and head towards the trees bordering the northwest corner of the cricket pitch. Here, a gap in the trees marks the start of a track – the gap is clear enough, though the track itself is a little hard to spot at the very edge of the wood; you should soon pick it up, though, behind the gnarled old tree dead ahead of you.

The track wriggles west for 500m before emerging at a lane. Turn right here and head uphill through **Nomansland village** – little more than a hamlet of half-timbered houses at the edge of the common – and on uphill towards **Amwell** village. At the southern limits of Amwell, 500m on from the common in a fork in the road, stands the *Elephant & Castle* **pub**.

The *Elephant & Castle* serves lunches from noon till 2pm on Monday to Saturday. It's a lovely old pub, with a large inglenook fireplace, stripped-back brickwork, wood panelling and tiled floors.

Catuvellaunian Britain

A hundred years before the arrival of the Romans, Britain was invaded by the **Catuvellauni** (meaning "expert warriors"), an aggressive warrior tribe from Belgium who, by the first century BC, had gained control of much of southern Britain, making **Oppidum**, just outside present-day Wheathampstead (and later Verlamion, outside St Albans) their capital. The Catuvellauni also had a hand in events on the continent, making raids back across the English Channel and assisting their kinsfolk, the Gauls, who were holding back the Roman armies in northern Europe.

So significant did **Julius Caesar** consider the Catuvellauni's influence in Gaul to be, that he launched an expedition across the English Channel and reputedly killed their king, Cassivallaunus, at Oppidum in 54 BC. With the Belgic tribe weakened, the Romans were able to seize Gaul and prepare their plans for an invasion of Britain – though in the event this was not to occur for a further century. The Catuvellauni were still a significant threat to the invading Roman army, however, so much so that one of the earliest fortifications in the area was within sight of the then Catuvellaunian capital, Verlamion, just outside present-day St Albans. (For more on this, see box on p.210.)

Amwell to the Lea Valley Way

2km

Take the left fork at the *Elephant & Castle* and continue 150m up this lane, then turn left at the public footpath sign opposite Weaver's Cottage, up a short series of steps to a track that runs straight on, along the edge of a golf course. The views across the Hertfordshire countryside open up here, with the hamlet of Ayres End, nestling 1km south on a wooded hillside, the only settlement in view to interrupt the undulating folds of the valley. At the end of the golf course, 300m from the lane, head straight on, through a gap in the hedge, and continue on along the waymarked path through the middle of fields and towards the buildings of **Pipers Stud Farm**, which flank the track to the left for 150m to Pipers Lane. Turn right onto the lane, past a clutch of large 1930s houses, heavily influenced by the Arts & Crafts movement – the first and smallest of the houses, the half-timbered and red-tiled **Pipers Croft**, is a typical example.

After 500m the lane ends at a T-junction with the main Harpenden Road. Cross straight over the road and carry straight on, following public footpath signs, over a stile and into a field beyond the hedgerow. Go diagonally across the field, heading down to the left to another stile just before a large barn. Cross the stile, turn right and go past the barn to a bend in the track opposite a metal kissing gate and a fingerpost sign, to rejoin the path we were on earlier in the walk.

Back to Harpenden station

3.5km

Retrace your steps from here, going back through the metal kissing gates down to Leasey Bridge, then along the track that flanks the southern bank of the River Lea into Harpenden. Turn right by the *Marquis of Granby* pub, then left, following the riverside track to come out at the weirs by the children's playground. Go along the pavement by the hawthorn hedge and up Station Road, from the bend by *The Dolphin* pub, to return to **Harpenden station**.

St Albans and around

St Albans via Verulamium to Gorhambury

Distance and difficulty: 15km; easy.
Train: King's Cross Thameslink to St Albans (every 15–20min; 20–30min); St Albans to King's Cross Thameslink (every 15–20min; 20–30min).
Map: OS Landranger 166: *Luton & Hertford*; OS Explorer 182: *St Albans & Hatfield*.

Starting in the historic cathedral city of **St Albans**, this gentle circular walk heads through the remains of **Verulamium**, once a major Roman city, and on to **Watling Street**, the great Roman road which ran from London to Chester. Leaving the old Roman city, the walk then continues out through the surrounding countryside to the village of **Gorhambury**, whose fine Georgian country house stands next to the picturesque Tudor ruins of an earlier manor. Beyond Gorhambury, there's a conveniently located pub, the *Hollybush*, which makes a good lunch stop. Alternatively, there are plenty of great **pubs** offering good grub in St Michael's, on the far side of Verulamium Park.

Note that the lane leading up to Gorhambury from Verulamium is a **permissive path** through private land rather than a public right of way, and is closed on 1 June each year, and on Saturdays from September to January.

Getting started

1km

From the northbound platform at St Albans **train station** (the one you arrive at from London), head straight through the ticket barrier across the small car park and out to the main road. Turn left up **Victoria Street**, passing Trinity Reformed Church at the crossroads on your right and a mishmash of bland twentieth-century office blocks and diminutive Victorian workers' cottages beyond, then follow the road as it climbs steeply towards the centre of affluent St Albans. At the top of the hill, the heart of the city is marked by the early nineteenth-century **town hall**, whose confident main facade, consisting of a giant first-floor portico punctuated by four fluted Ionic columns, overlooks the town's wide principal drag, St Peter's Street. The lobby is now home to the city's **tourist office** (Easter–Oct Mon–Sat 9.30am–5.30pm; Nov–Easter Mon–Sat 9am–4pm; ☏ 01727/864511, ⓦ www.stalbans.gov.uk).

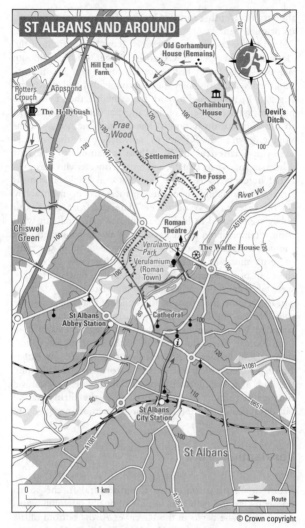

From the town hall to the cathedral

0.5km

St Albans is at its bustling best on a Saturday, when the area in front of the town hall and the streets around it are filled with **market stalls** selling everything from fruit and veg to antiques. Victoria Street ends at a T-junction with St Peter's Street at the side of the town hall. Cross St Peter's Street and head past the town hall, taking the road that leads downhill on its far side. You're now in the heart of medieval St Albans, with its ancient brick-and-flint and half-timbered buildings (most now converted into shops) and the cheery pubs of Market Place. Between them stands the city's fifteenth-century **Curfew Tower**, complete with its original bell.

Head down pedestrianized French Row, to the right of the clock tower, to reach busy **George Street**. On the opposite side of George Street, just to the left of the pedestrian crossing, there's a narrow alley; head through this and down the flagstoned path beyond towards the cathedral, then follow the path around the east end of the cathedral (left and then right) to the entrance on its south side. Overlooking grassy lawns sloping down to the River Ver – now little more than a trickle – the **Cathedral of St Alban** is named for the first Christian martyr in Britain, a Roman convert who was executed here in 209 AD. The vast flint and brick building is largely Norman in origin, though there has been an abbey on this site since Saxon times. Materials from the Saxon abbey were reused to build the Norman cathedral, but what is most telling about the materials used in the construction of the cathedral is their striking similarity to those in the ruins of Verulamium; like much of the city that grew up outside the ruins of the Roman city, raw materials – flint and brick – were taken from the earlier site and recycled here.

Inside, it's the sheer size of the building that impresses: the cathedral has the longest medieval nave in the country. The rounded Norman arches and pillars are, again, clearly built from Roman brick (though those to the south are later additions, elaborate Decorated structures that replace the earlier Norman ones, which collapsed in a storm in 1323). Behind the high altar lies the **tomb of St Alban** – its pedestal is a nineteenth-century reconstruction, since the shrine was all but destroyed during the Dissolution. For more on St Alban, see the box on p.210.

Verulamium Park

1km

From the main entrance to the cathedral in the south transept, take the path that heads diagonally downhill across the lawns to the banks of the River Ver. At the bottom of the path, on the river bank, is **Ye Olde Fighting Cocks** pub, which claims to be the oldest pub in Britain. Whether or not it is (a dozen other places across the country make the same claim), the pretty, higgledy-piggledy inn has been here since at least 1600 and once hosted Oliver Cromwell. In summer you can sit out on benches by the river. A few metres beyond, a red-brick footbridge spans the river and leads you into Verulamium Park.

Verulamium Park, complete with two ornamental lakes and a host of ducks and geese, occupies the southern half of the site of the walled Roman town of **Verulamium** (see box on p.210) – the River Ver marked the city's eastern boundary. You'll see the extensive remains of various other parts of the city throughout the walk. Bear right immediately beyond the bridge and follow the path that leads between the Ver on your right and the ornamental lakes on your left; from here you can see a small stretch of Roman wall on the far side of the lake.

Through St Michael's

0.3km

Head straight through the park and out onto the high street of **St Michael's**, a small eighteenth-century village which has now been absorbed into the city's outlying suburbs. Bear left and head up past the *Rose & Crown* and *Six Bells* pubs, both of which serve **lunch** and have small beer gardens (the former's is more appealing). The street rises gradually uphill then bears right.

The *Waffle House* (daily: Easter–Oct 10am–6pm; Oct–Easter 10am–5pm) in the former Kingsbury Mill, on the banks of the River Ver in St Michael's, makes for a good lunch or afternoon-tea stop, serving sweet and savoury American-style waffles, plus teas and coffee.

A small road continues up to the left. Detour up here to reach the excellent **Verulamium Museum** (Mon–Sat 10am–5.30pm, Sun 2–5.30pm; £3). This well-put-together museum offers a fascinating insight into life in Roman Britain, with computer-generated "walk-throughs" of the Roman town and plenty of other gadgets and gizmos to entertain the lay person, as well as trays of finds for the more archeologically minded. The highlight is the collection of five remarkably complete floor **mosaics**; these were a status symbol in middle-class Roman society. The mosaics were all unearthed locally, and date from around 200 AD.

The Roman Theatre

0.2km

Continuing up St Michael's Street from the turn-off to Verulamium Museum brings you after 50m to a T-junction with the busy A4147, some 200m from the turn-off to the museum. Cross to the far side and head down the private road opposite, past a lodge house, following signs for the **Roman Theatre**. The remains of the theatre (daily 10am–4 or 5pm; £1.50) sit in the field to the right of this private road; tickets are sold at the small booth 50m from the main road. The theatre stood on **Watling Street**, the main axis of the Roman town, and several tiers of the original building are clearly visible, though the columns on the stage are modern replicas, added to give a sense of scale to the ruins. You can also take a look at several Roman workshops, currently under excavation just south of the theatre.

Roman Verulamium and St Alban

Following the fall of southern Britain to the advancing Roman armies in 43 AD, the invaders quickly established a fort on the banks of the River Ver, in the present-day suburb of St Michael's. The Romans were attracted not only by the site's strategic location, but also by its symbolic significance, since it stood just northeast of the former Belgic town **Verlamion**, capital of the Catuvellauni a tribe which Julius Caesar had quashed a century earlier (see box on p.204). Within five years, the original fort had begun to expand into a prosperous Roman town, and **Verulamium**, as the new settlement became known, quickly developed into an important trading post on the London–Chester and Colchester–Silchester Roman roads. Despite being sacked by **Boudicca** in 79 AD and razed by fire in AD 155, Verulamium remained an important Roman town until the fourth century, when it was finally abandoned by the retreating Roman armies. Some Roman civilians stayed on, however, and the remains of a middle-class villa dating from this time stands to the north of the city walls in the grounds of Gorhambury.

During the Roman period, the new religion of **Christianity** began to grow in popularity, despite being outlawed by Rome; in 209 AD, **Alban**, a Roman convert from Verulamium, become the first Christian martyr in England. The site of Alban's execution, on the hillside overlooking the town to the northeast, developed into a shrine during Roman times, then later a church and an abbey after the Romans had left. The religious buildings were made from materials pilfered from the abandoned town at the foot of the hill. The abbey was massively extended by the Norman abbot, **Paul of Caen**, in 1077, and the present-day cathedral has changed little since that time.

By 948 AD, records show that market traders were allowed to set up stalls just outside the abbey precinct, marking the beginning of the market town that grew up on the hill around the shrine to St Alban, from which it took its name. Like the abbey, the town buildings were largely made from reclaimed bricks from the Roman site, something which is particularly noticeable in the heart of the medieval city, where flint and brick houses predominate.

Through Gorhambury Park

5km

The gate beyond the ticket booth marks the start of Gorhambury Walk, which leads up through **Gorhambury Park** to Gorhambury House. Initially taking the course of the tree-lined road ahead, the walk follows the route of **Watling Street**, the Roman road that ran from London via Verulamium to the great Roman city of Deva (now Chester) on the Welsh border; there's little in the way of evidence of the Roman road here today, though its course is clearly marked on Ordnance Survey maps. These also show the surrounding countryside to be dotted with Roman and pre-Roman remains – these include small temples; Roman fortifications protecting Verulamium ("The Fosse" on the maps); a post-Verulamium Roman villa (a short way north of the track); and Verlamion, a first-century BC stronghold of the Catuvellauni, a Belgic tribe who dominated the southeast prior to the Roman invasions (it's up in Prae Wood to your left). Unfortunately, all these lie in the private grounds off the track, so you can't visit them.

Gorhambury Walk is open daily from 8am to 6pm, except from September to January, when it's closed on Saturdays. Dogs must be kept on leads.

It's the walk's rural attractions – and great views back to the city and cathedral – that are the principal appeal hereabouts. Beyond the Roman Theatre, fields run down to the River Ver, while Prae Wood blankets the hillside above the excavated site, and ahead Maynes Farm stands at a bend in the road. After around 1.5km, the road passes a turn-off for the Ver Valley Walk and begins to climb uphill and away from the course of Watling Street, which formerly ran on through the fields to your right – though it's marked on the Ordnance Survey maps, there's nothing to see of the Roman road here today. On the rise to the left, elegant Gorhambury House (see below) appears through a break in the trees. Head on past Maynes Farm, and follow the drive as it sweeps up past Nash Lodge (once part of the Gorhambury estate, but now a private home) and onto the final gravel approach to Gorhambury House. The wooded grounds slope down to the right towards **Prae Wood**, which shelters the earthworks of the first-century Celtic settlement of **Verlamion**, the very first recorded town in this area and the one that gave both the nearby River Ver and the Roman city their names. The site was the capital of a Belgic tribe, the Catuvellauni, who also had a major settlement outside present-day Wheathampstead.

Continue up the gravel approach, then follow the path round behind **Gorhambury House** and past the stables and paddock. Built in the late eighteenth century, the house's creamy white facade is of Portland stone, fronted by a Corinthian portico. The house takes its name from Geoffrey de Gorham, the Abbot of St Albans from 1119 to 1146, who had had the first manor house built here on what was then abbey land. Gorhambury House is open one day a week in summer (May–Sept Thurs only 2–5pm; small fee); exhibits include family portraits, handmade carpets, Chippendale furniture and the like – interesting enough, though you're really not missing too much if you don't manage to turn up when it's open.

Beyond the house, the path snakes past modern estate buildings before turning a corner and giving you your first view of the romantic ruins of old **Gorhambury Manor**, an unexpected sight, since you're almost on top of the house before you see them. The estate was sold off following the dissolution of the monasteries, and a generation later fell into the hands of Sir Nicholas Bacon, father of Francis and lord chancellor to Elizabeth I. In 1568 Bacon senior constructed the house whose ruins you now see, reusing remains from Verulamium and the abbey buildings at St Albans. Sir Francis Bacon inherited the estate when his father died, but with no heir of his own to pass the property on to, he gave Gorhambury to his secretary, who later sold it to the Grimston family who still live here today. The Grimstons later commissioned new Gorhambury House after the family outgrew the Tudor manor, later pulling down the old house to create a romantic ruin. The remains – the crumbling porch and part of the red-brick and flint hall – are today managed by English Heritage (free access). An inscription over the entrance commemorates the fact that it was built in the tenth year of Elizabeth I's reign, although following her first visit to the house, she complained that it wasn't big enough, forcing Sir Nicholas to have the building extended.

From old Gorhambury House, the drive heads downhill, past **Temple Cottage**, named after a Roman temple that once stood nearby, which has a portico echoing that of the big house, and then past Stud Farm and some cottages before reaching a gate that marks the end of the private road. Head straight on up the public road, past Hill End Farm, and through an underpass beneath the M10 to return to the busy A4147.

To Potters Crouch

1.5km

After the bucolic surroundings of the last 5km, the noise of these busy roads comes as a brief but unwelcome intrusion. There are **buses** (every 10–15min) back into St Albans from the stop just to the left of you as you reach the main road, but the **walk** back through the country lanes on the opposite side of the A4147 is pleasant enough, once you've put the roads behind you after around 500m.

Cross the main road and head down **Appspond Lane**, which flanks the M1 motorway for a few hundred metres before veering away and heading past the clutch of half a dozen whitewashed cottages that constitute the hamlet of **Appspond** and on into the small village of **Potters Crouch**, just under 2km from the A4147. The village is typical of the local architecture, with black weatherboarded houses with red-tiled roofs. The lane ends at a T-junction in the village. Turn left here and head through the village to *The Hollybush* pub, then follow Rugged Hall Lane off to the right, passing Potters Crouch East Farm, complete with duck pond.

Back to St Albans

5.5km

Just under 1km from Potters Crouch you pass **Park Wood** on your left. Beyond it, a waymarked path leads off to the left. Head up this for 500m, flanking the side of the wood at the edges of Westfield's Farm, to reach a footbridge over the M10 motorway, just beyond an ugly phone mast. On the far side of the motorway, a well-maintained track heads downhill across a field to the modern sprawl of St Albans. The track cuts north through a 1970s housing estate to come out after 1km at a pedestrian crossing on **King Harry Lane**. Cross the lane to reach the path directly opposite, which leads down and over a wooden footbridge across the ditch fortifications to the city of Verulamium.

You are now at the southwest corner of Verulamium Park, equivalent to the southwest corner of the Roman city and boasting the impressive remains of the brick and flint **Roman wall**, which flanks the modern footpath all the way down to the lawns above the park's ornamental lakes. Near the bottom of this path, you pass the remains of the **London Gate**, Verulamium's main southern entrance, where Watling Street ran into the city.

Carry straight on down the path and past the ornamental lakes to reach the bridge by *Ye Olde Fighting Cocks* pub and retrace your steps back up past the cathedral, through the town centre and down Victoria Street to **St Albans train station**.

Woburn Safari Park
Aspley Guise to Woburn Village

Distance and difficulty: 15km, plus optional 6km detour; moderate.

Train: Euston to Bletchley (every 30min; 50min–1hr), then Bletchley to Aspley Guise (Mon–Sat 1 hourly; 15min); alternatively, St Pancras to Bedford (hourly; 30min) or King's Cross Thameslink to Bedford (every 15min; 1hr), then Bedford to Aspley Guise (Mon–Sat 1 hourly; 30min). There are no services to Aspley Guise on Sundays.

Maps: OS Landranger 153 and 165: *Bedford and Huntington* and *Aylesbury & Leighton Buzzard*; OS Explorer 192: *Buckingham & Milton Keynes*.

Starting in the village of **Aspley Guise**, this circular walk takes you through the **Woburn Estate**, seat of the dukes of Bedford since the seventeenth century and now home to **Woburn Safari Park** – the country's largest – as well as the stately family home, **Woburn Abbey**, named for the monastery that once stood here. The walk loops round the safari park before heading over the hill to cross the estate's **deer park** and past the abbey itself; an optional six-kilometre loop leads around the abbey and through landscaped **Woburn Park**. From the abbey, it's a short walk out to the attractive, largely Georgian, village of **Woburn**, which has several good **pubs** – the pretty, whitewashed and thatched *Royal Oak* is the most conveniently located. The walk back to Aspley Guise takes you through farmland and along lanes to the medieval heart of the village; alternatively, if you want to shorten the walk you can take a taxi back to Aspley Guise train station from Woburn or a bus to Bletchley (or Leighton Buzzard, which is also on the Euston–Bletchley train line).

Getting started
1km

From **Aspley Guise station**, head up the lane (across the level crossing if you're coming from Bletchley; or turn left straight off the platform if you're coming from Bedford) into Aspley Guise. The heart of the village itself lies 1km ahead, beyond the wooded hill. A few metres from the station, the road begins to snake up the side of this hill, passing whitewashed Victorian workers' cottages and heading up to the village's medieval church, whose Perpendicular tower peeps up above the trees on the brow of the hill. **St Botolph**'s was heavily restored by the Victorians – in fact the whole south aisle was built in 1855 – but the exterior restoration, at least, has been essentially sympathetic to the medieval period.

A few metres beyond the church, at a bend in the road just before a high red-brick wall, turn left and head through a metal kissing gate, following the public footpath signs onto a dirt track that leads gently downhill to Bedford Road. The track flanks the northern wall of **Aspley House**, giving views across formal gardens of the eighteenth-century house's elegant red-brick exterior. To your left is a small meadow, swathed with snowdrops and daffodils in spring.

Aspley Guise to the Woburn Estate
2km

The dirt track ends at another kissing gate at the Bedford Road. Turn left here, cross the road at the central reservation a few metres on, then continue along the far side of the road, passing the Tudor half-timbered and thatched **Park** and **Valentine cottages**. Just beyond the cottages, turn right onto **Mount Pleasant**, a quiet lane that leads up past *The Wheatsheaf* pub (hot and cold bar snacks) and rows of tiny Victorian workers' cottages and larger Georgian houses to the village limits, where Mount Pleasant becomes **Horsepool Lane**. This runs gently downhill between fields and past a small copse before reaching a cluster of gabled red-brick houses at a T-junction on the A4012, 1.5km beyond *The Wheatsheaf*.

Woburn Safari Park
2.5km

A few metres to the right, on the opposite side of the road, is one of the entrances to **Woburn Safari Park**. Go through the metal gates at the entrance to the park, following the yellow waymarkers; the first is a few metres on, beyond a gnarled oak tree to the left of the drive. Carry straight on, following the path as it runs between wire fencing through a scrubby, run-down corner of the estate. Some 200m from the entrance you reach a small wooden stile. Turn right here to reach an access road a few metres further on. The yellow waymarkers are a little confusing: on the opposite side of the access road there's a dirt track up past a woodcutter's hut up wooded Dean Hills; ignore the yellow waymarker directing you up here. Instead turn right and head along the tarred access road itself; the yellow waymarkers resume after 100m or so.

The road runs below wooded **Dean Hills**, which rise to your left, while rhododendrons border the roadside. Some 700m along the access road, just before a bend, turn left along a grassy waymarked track which follows the bottom of the hills; the track runs parallel to the road, 50m or so to the left of the **Leisure Area** (you'll see a children's adventure playground through the trees to your right). Of more interest to walkers is the animal life you'll see all around: you'll often see rabbits on the wooded hillside, as well as some of the thousands of deer that live on the estate here.

Follow the grassy track for 600m. Just before the access road by some functional-looking wooden maintenance buildings turn left, following the waymarked track uphill through the woods that cover the flanks of Dean Hills. At the top of the hill, a five-step stile leads out of the trees and onto the top of the hills. Below to your right you'll get your first view of the **safari park** itself.

The path continues along the hilltop for 700m, giving uninterrupted views into the park. You're pretty much guaranteed to see elephants, zebras, tigers, lions or rhinos, all of which live in the enclosures here, and it's an unforgettably surreal sight to see the stately Asian elephants walking majestically through the Bedfordshire countryside. This section of track ends at a large wooden kissing gate by Crawleyheath Farm, right by the **main entrance** to the park. Turn right and go through the farm, past a red telephone box and over the main approach to the park, flanked by two lion sculptures, then head for the metal gates in the fence opposite at the boundary of Brickground Plantation, a wooded hill that rises above the entrance to the Safari Park.

On to Woburn Abbey

4km

There are no waymarkers beyond the gate at Crawleyheath Farm until you head into the woods of **Brickground Plantation**. From the gates through the plantation's wire boundary fence, bear right towards the no entry sign by the maintenance hut and you'll soon see the waymarkers just to the left of this private access track, directing you up the wide dirt track into the trees via a dilapidated wooden gate.

At the top of the hill you come to an access road, just to the right of a large whitewashed cottage and a gated entrance at the edge of Woburn's Deer Park. Head over the double stiles to the left of the cattle grid and then go straight on, following the footpath which runs along the left side of the road. The path heads straight along the high ground for 500m or so, passing **The Thornery**, a tiny thatched stone cottage just north of the safari park boundary on your right. You can see across to Dean Hills here, beyond the safari park, but next to nothing of the park itself, although the grassy hilltop to your left is a popular spot with the estate's deer.

Just beyond a tiny pond, a few metres beyond The Thornery, and by a small white "No Pedestrian Access" sign, the waymarkers begin to lead you away from the access road and downhill towards the red-brick chimney-tops of houses just outside the estate, beyond another access gate. At the access gate, turn right and head uphill, following the waymarkers on the far side of the road. Some 200m from the

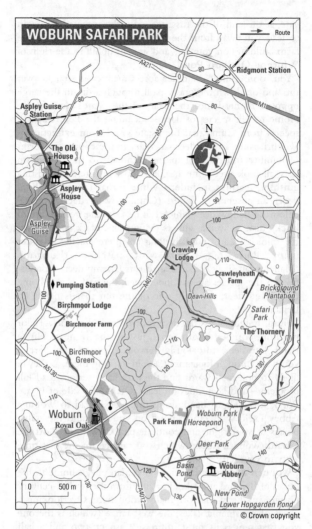

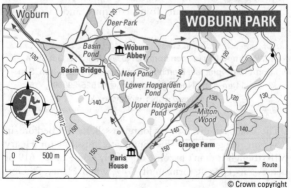

gate, at the end of the first steep rise, the waymarkers begin to lead you away from the road, over an access road to the farm buildings on your left, and straight uphill to the right of **Whitnoe Orchard Pond**.

You soon come to another access road; cross straight over this and on down the grassy path through a dip in the verge opposite to head into the heart of the estate's **deer park**. Home to ten species of deer – including the Père David, a species from China that the estate saved from extinction – Woburn is the largest deer sanctuary in the country in terms of number and types of species, although to the lay person they all look pretty much alike. If you're interested, distinguishing features include: a white throat (Axis or Chital deer); an absence of antlers (Chinese water deer); unusual colouring (fallow deer, which can be anything from white to black); tusks as well as antlers (Muntjac); a black stripe down the spine plus an unusually long tail (Père David); a winter mane (Rusa stags); large white patch on the rump (Manchurian sika); or bat-shaped ears (swamp deer). In addition to the species already mentioned, the park is also home to the red deer, the only one of the ten that is native to Britain.

Head straight across the deer park towards the mock-Tudor pavilion, complete with moat, just to the right of Horse Pond. The deer, notoriously nervous creatures, will part as you walk through their midst. Avoid startling them, as they're likely to bolt road-wards, and the park has a serious road-kill problem – and keep dogs on leads. On the far side of Horse Pond, turn left to head along the access road to Woburn Abbey itself, with Horse Pond on your left and the stable blocks to your right, and continue past **Cowmans Cottage** towards Woburn Abbey, which you can see for the first time away to your left.

Woburn Abbey, a grandiose Georgian pile, is home to the dukes of Bedford and takes its name from the twelfth-century Cistercian abbey that originally stood here. Overlooking a series of ornamental lakes, the west range (which is the one you first see) is its most impressive aspect: two and a half storeys high, with giant Ionic columns, and faced with creamy white stone.

Woburn Abbey is open from Jan to late March & Oct Sat & Sun 11am–4pm; late March to Sept Mon–Sat 11am–4pm, Sun 11am–5pm; Nov & Dec closed; ⊤ 01525/290666, ⓦ www.woburnabbey.co.uk.

The estate was given to Sir John Russell, Earl of Bedford, in 1547 in recognition of his diplomatic missions for Henry VIII, though it didn't become the family home until 1619 or achieve its current form until 1747, when Henry Flitcroft was commissioned by the fourth duke to build the west range. Inside, Flitcroft's lavish staterooms are lined with paintings by artists including Gainsborough, Van Dyck and Reynolds. The **grounds** were landscaped in 1802, by Henry Repton who introduced the series of ornamental ponds that now stand before the house.

Detour around Woburn Park

6km

This additional circuit of **Woburn Park** is a good afternoon extension to the main walk, though it makes for a very long day, unless you catch a bus or taxi back from Woburn.

From Cowmans Cottage, follow the drive past Repton's ornamental ponds and up to the brow of the hill, just before the abbey house and gardens; there are good views here down to **Basin Pond**, the largest of the ornamental ponds, which stands directly in front of the house. At the brow of the hill, turn left and head up through the visitors' car park and along the road that flanks the landscaped gardens behind the house.

At a bend in the road, 500m from the car park, head straight on over the grass, following stubby yellow waymarkers downhill and through the trees towards a gate at the edge of a new plantation of fir trees. Head through the gate and over the stile and along the grassy path through this plantation to a stile 100m further on at the opposite end; this leads down into the more established pine-tree copse on **Purretts Hill**.

The path continues through the copse on Purretts Hill and emerges on its south side, then continues over a field to the tree-fringed ornamental **Linden Lake**; to the right, a small bamboo plantation thrives in the marshy ground around the lake. Go over the stile at the bottom of the field and then cross the plank bridge over the first tributary; head over the grass and on to a second plank bridge to cross the next ditch, then turn right by the waymarker post and head south through the trees and over a stile and through the bamboo plantation to the edge of **Milton Woods** ahead of you.

A few metres to the right of the path out of the bamboo there's a small gap in the hedgerow, where you'll find a bridge over the ditch which leads to a wide dirt track through the western edge of the woods; to your right is the high red-brick wall that marks the boundary of the Woburn Estate. Carry straight on over a stile at the far end of the wood and along a track at the bottom of a field, passing a reed bed in the marshy ground to your right. Just beyond here, you come to a T-junction with a track up to Grange Farm to your left; turn right to follow this track away from the farm, over a ditch round to the left and along by the red-brick boundary wall to your right. After about 100m you pass through a wooden gate at the corner of a field. Continue straight ahead for 70m; on your right you'll see a gap in the trees and a little footbridge over the ditch, leading through the trees to a gate in the brick wall a few metres ahead.

Go through the gate, which takes you back into the estate by **Paris House**, a large, mock-Tudor Victorian house. Keeping the boundary wall of Paris House to your left, head up to the access road and then straight on down it. Some 50m further on you pass a ring of trees on your left, marking the boundary of a small reservoir, and the ruins of a round-house to your right. Beyond here, the route heads downhill towards Woburn Abbey, passing the highest of the ornamental ponds, over to your right, and heading down towards the largest of them, Basin Pond, right in front of the house.

Go along the road almost to the bridge over the narrow northern end of Basin Pond. A few metres before it, turn left and follow the stumpy yellow waymarkers through the trees, keeping Basin Pond to your right and heading back through the deer park to a high metal kissing gate just to the right of an enclosed wooded copse. This is the exit out of the estate towards Woburn village.

Woburn village

1km

Whether or not you decide to do the six-kilometre detour around Woburn Park, you'll need to exit the estate through the high metal kissing gate mentioned above. If you've skipped the additional loop, you get to the gate by carrying on along the dirt track that begins at the bend in the road a few metres beyond Cowmans Cottage and Horse Pond (see p.218; note that the no entry sign here applies to cars only). This track leads beneath **Shoulder of Mutton** pond, whose steep retaining banks hide the water from sight for the first 50m. Carry straight on, passing a small brick maintenance hut on your right, to reach the edge of a wooded area and the aforementioned large metal kissing gate. Go through the kissing gate and head down the dirt track between fields to your right and woods to your left, both bounded by high wire fencing. After 200m you reach another high kissing gate to the right of the red-sandstone **Ivy Lodge**.

Beyond this second kissing gate, turn right and follow the footpath alongside the A4012 for a few hundred metres into **Woburn village**. This attractive place has a predominantly Georgian character (much of the village was destroyed by fire in 1720, and promptly rebuilt in the style of the day), with tiny cottages lining the wide streets through which drovers once took their sheep to the thrice weekly market. There are several **pubs** here: the first you come to is the whitewashed and thatched *Royal Oak* on George Street (as the A4012 is known as it enters the village).

> The *Royal Oak* serves lunches from noon to 3pm on weekdays
> and meals all day at weekends.

Back to Aspley Guise station

4.5km

If you want to end the walk here, you can take one of the
buses (1–2 hourly till around 3.30pm) from Woburn to
Leighton Buzzard from the bus stop just beyond Market
Place (see below) or a **taxi** back to Aspley Guise (around
£10; call ☏01908/646565). To walk back to Aspley Guise
station, head straight through the village along the A4012,
passing the village's tiny **Market Place**, just beyond a crossroads, and heading out of the village some 500m beyond the
Royal Oak pub. Ignore the first (main) right-hand turn just
outside the village, and take the second (minor) road 200m
further on. Follow this road straight on through the tiny
hamlet of **Birchmoor Green**, 100m beyond the turn-off,
and then along the dirt track where the road ends, just
beyond the village up towards a red-brick Elizabethan farmhouse to **Birchmoor Farm**.

At the hedgerow parallel with the farm buildings, turn right
onto another, waymarked, path that takes you up to the
entrance to the farmhouse, then left down its drive towards
Birchmoor Lodge. Here, you come out onto narrow Aspley
Lane; turn right and follow the lane for 800m, passing a small
Victorian pumping station and passing a left-hand turn
towards Woburn Sands. From this point on there are white
fingerposts directing you uphill into Aspley Guise, which
you'll reach after 1km. Cross the main road and head up the
road to the right of the tiny village green; after 500m you'll
reach **St Botolph's church**; continue straight on to **Aspley
Guise station**.

9

Essex, Cambridge and the Fens

D ue north of London, the university town of **Cambridge** makes a well-established day-trip from London, and needs little introduction here. By contrast, the rural fringes of Essex, to the south of Cambridge, and the flat fenlands to its north, are relatively little visited. This is a shame, since despite its brash reputation, **Essex** remains one of the least built-up of the home counties, and still boasts handsome market towns set in acres of unspoilt countryside. North of Cambridge, the bleak **fenlands** provide a startling contrast with the cosy walks covered in the rest of this chapter, offering a landscape that is harsh but strangely beautiful, with vast, perfectly flat fields of rich, peat-black soil, framed by immense skies.

The first of the walks in this chapter goes from Bishop's Stortford to Sawbridgeworth along the **River Stort**, once used to transport barley from the surrounding farmland to malting houses down the river, and still busy with pleasure boats. Further north, the second walk heads out to **Saffron Walden**, a Saxon market town that made its name – and much of its wealth – from the saffron crocus that once grew in abundance here, and the nearby stately home of **Audley End**. From Cambridge, the third walk makes the short trip south to **Grantchester** along the River Cam, where punters head in summer and Rupert Brooke and his bohemian chums hung out between the two world wars. North of Cambridge, a two-day walk heads north through the fens along the Fen Rivers Way from Waterbeach, just north of Cambridge, to **Ely**, whose cathedral dominates the skyline from miles around.

The area has good **train** links to London. Two of the four walks in this chapter begin and end at stations on the **Liverpool Street** to Cambridge line, though for Cambridge itself (and also for Ely) there are faster services from **King's Cross**. It takes around an hour to reach Cambridge and Ely; thirty to forty minutes to get to the beginning of the Essex walks. Virtually all these trains stop either at Finsbury Park (from King's Cross) or Tottenham Hale (Liverpool Street). Ely is the furthest flung and longest of these walks, and you'll need plenty of time to include the detour to Wicken Fen; aim to start walking by 10.30am.

Along the River Stort

Bishop's Stortford to Sawbridgeworth

Distance and difficulty: 8.5km; moderate.
Train: Liverpool Street to Bishop's Stortford (every 30min; 35–55min); return from Sawbridgeworth to Liverpool Street (1–2 hourly; 40–50min).
Map: OS Landranger 167: *Chelmsford*; OS Explorer 195 and 194: *Braintree & Saffron Walden* and *Hertford & Bishop's Stortford*.

Straddling the Hertfordshire–Essex border, the **River Stort** was an important navigable waterway during the Industrial Revolution, used chiefly to transport barley from local farms to malt houses along the riverbanks. East Hertfordshire, in particular, was an important brewing centre, as were neighbouring Essex towns such as Bishop's Stortford.

Starting at the handsome market town of **Bishop's Stortford**, midway between London and Cambridge, this walk follows the **River Stort** as it meanders its way south via lock houses and through pastureland and reed-filled floodplains to the impressive eighteenth-century maltings at **Sawbridgeworth**. Now a wealthy commuter town, Sawbridgeworth maintained a steady prosperity on the back of the brewing industry right up until the late nineteenth century. Fittingly, given its history, the town claims to have more pubs per capita than anywhere else in the country, meaning that there are plenty of choices for **lunch**.

Getting started

0.75km

Take the main exit out of **Bishop's Stortford station** and follow the slip road up to a T-junction. Turn right here and cross the bridge over the railway, and then right again onto the busy A1060, following the rail tracks for a few hundred metres up to a roundabout. Bear right here along the minor road that crosses back over the railway and loops down past the *Tanners Arms* pub to the **River Stort**.

Here, the river briefly flanks the south side of the road before veering off to the south; take the path that follows the riverside, passing the backs of houses and some small-scale warehousing. After 100m, just beyond the bridge under the railway, you come to a wooden footbridge over a **weir** – the first of many along the navigable river, which help control the levels of water in it, siphoning excess volume into backwaters, reed beds, marshes or floodplains.

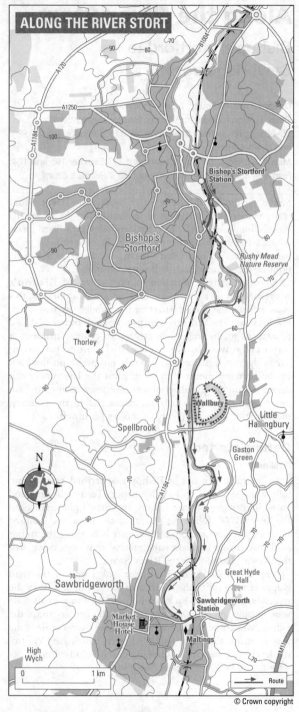

ALONG THE RIVER STORT

© Crown copyright

Southmill Lock to Twyford Lock

1.75km

A few metres beyond the weir is the first of the five locks which dot the walk: **Southmill Lock**. Now used exclusively by pleasure boats, these traditional locks, with their well-kept lock houses, form an attractive feature of the river. Cross the lock gates to the left bank of the river (which you continue to follow for the remainder of the walk). About 500m beyond here, a sign to the left of the path marks the first of two entrances to the **Rushy Mead Nature Reserve**, a 11.5 acre conservation area which protects part of the Stort flood-plain. The reserve covers three different wetland habitats – open water, reed and sedge beds – and a host of aquatic wildlife, including reed warblers, snipes and willow tits, which lives in and around them; information boards throughout the reserve explain which types of plant and wildlife you can expect to see. It's possible to make the complete circuit of Rushy Mead – little more than 500m – and pick up the walk a few hundred metres further along the river.

About a kilometre further on, less than 50m beyond the second entrance to the reserve, the path passes the straggling end of Bishop's Stortford, running beside large houses whose long gardens back on to the path. Though it's hard to believe it from the bucolic scenery in the near distance, the bulk of the town lies less than 500m off to the right of the river. It's not until the next lock – **Twyford** – a few hundred metres further on, that the town is truly left behind.

At Twyford Lock, the river passes under a minor road over which you must cross to regain the towpath, through a kissing gate a little to your left on the far side of the road; the path directly ahead only leads down to a jetty. Passing by pasture land, the path soon rejoins the left riverbank.

Past Wallbury to Tednambury Lock

3km

Beyond Twyford Lock, the river meanders through open countryside, where horses are paddocked and cattle graze. A little under 2km further on it passes under a white bridge, from where a road leads up towards the northern flank of **Wallbury**, a Celtic hillfort that looms above the east bank of the river. Little is known about the original inhabitants of Wallbury, though Iron Age pottery has been recovered from the 30-acre site. The oval-shaped fort was defended by double ramparts and ditches; the original entrance can still be seen on the east side; today, the defences are heavily wooded and it's difficult to make out much of the original earthworks apart from the moat-like ditches that lie immediately below the towpath to your left. Around 500m beyond the white bridge, Wallbury ends at the third lock: **Spellbrook**.

Around 500m beyond Spellbrook, a long, sweeping bend in the river belies the even deeper sweep of river which runs behind it in a wooded copse; the river formerly followed this river bend, but the navigable Stort found a more direct route south along the long curve you can see ahead of you. The towpath follows the navigable stretch, crossing each end of the deeper river bend by way of two small bridges, 200m apart. Between the two is **Tednambury Lock**.

Beyond the second of these bridges, the river sweeps round, running close by the railway, with marshy fields and reed beds to the left, fed by two small weirs which siphon water from the river. The path is quite narrow in places, and you'll probably spend more time watching your feet than admiring the views, but look out for the abundant plant life, including blackberries and rosehips that line the way in summer.

Sawbridgeworth

3km

Just under 2km beyond Tednambury Lock the river passes under a low railway bridge and comes out on the northern outskirts of **Sawbridgeworth**. At the last of the five locks – **Sawbridgeworth Lock** – cross over the access road (which leads off to the right to the lock houses) and continue straight on, along the left bank of the river, passing the backs of large houses, whose gardens run down to the far river bank. After a few hundred metres you come out on the road by some old malt houses; Sawbridgeworth's tiny **train station** lies a few hundred metres beyond them, to your left.

You can return to London from here, but it's worth having a look round the sprawling **antiques shops** in the old malt houses, where there's also a tiny **café**. Alternatively, walk up into the town centre, a few hundred metres up the hill to your right, for a great **pub meal**. Head straight up The Forebury, the road at the bend to your right, which leads past a tiny green and a churchyard and up to the *Queen's Head* pub and *Market House Hotel*, to the left on the corner with Bell Street.

The cosy *Market House Hotel* has a large inglenook fireplace and low, oak-beamed ceilings; it serves great Sunday lunches and has a long list of specials at weekends.

To the station

2km

Two kilometres down London Road from Audley End house, turn right at the road sign for **Wendens Ambo** village and **Audley End train station**. Take the first turning left in Wendens Ambo to get to the station itself.

Along the Cam

Cambridge to Grantchester

Distance and difficulty: 12.5km; easy.
Train: King's Cross or Liverpool Street to Cambridge (every
30min from each station; 1hr–1hr 30min); return from Cambridge
to King's Cross or Liverpool Street (every 30min to both stations;
1hr–1hr 30min).
Map: OS Landranger 154: *Cambridge & Newmarket*; OS Explorer
209: *Cambridge*.

This walk heads south from **Cambridge** along the bank of
the **River Cam** to the halcyon village of **Grantchester**, little more than a high street, with a church, a green and rustic
thatched cottages. Grantchester has long been a popular day-
trip from the city, and it's still *de rigueur* for local undergradu-
ates to pack a picnic, rent a punt and spend a lazy summer's
day on the river here. *The Orchard House Tearooms*, right on
the river and with its own moorings, makes a good spot for
lunch or afternoon tea. There are also several good **pubs** in
the village, all offering bar meals. The return leg of the walk
heads north into Cambridge via **The Backs**, the lawns
behind the city's colleges from where there are superlative
views of the city. Past the Backs, the route returns via leafy
backstreets to the city's train station.

Getting started

1km

From **Cambridge station**, head straight up Station Road,
bear right onto Hills Road, cross over to the far side at the
pedestrian crossing and take the first turning left onto quiet,
leafy Bateman Street. At the far end of Bateman Street, cross
busy Trumpington Road at the pedestrian crossing and head
left down Trumpington Road for 100m, past Belvoir Terrace
to reach the edge of a meadow. Turn right here and follow a
tarred path off to the right.

Coe Fen and Paradise Nature Reserve

1.5km

Follow the path round the back of Belvoir Terrace and head
north along the right bank of a small brook. After a few hundred metres you'll reach a pair of metal footbridges marking
the southern reaches of **Coe Fen**, a marshy area on the banks
of the River Cam. Too soft to be of use for building, the land
was historically used as free grazing land for local people, and
cows, sheep and even horses are still left here to keep the
grass trim and to encourage wild flowers to grow.

museum inside about the Lord Protector's ten-year sojourn here (open daily in summer 10am–5.30pm; winter Mon–Sat 10am–5.30pm & Sun 11am–3pm; £3.50).

Take the path from the gate of St Mary's across the grass to the Cambridge Road. Go over at the pedestrian crossing, then turn right and sharp left along **Downham Road**, following the green footpath sign for the Bishop's Way. After a few minutes, Downham Road bears off to the right and West Fen Road continues west towards the A10. Follow West Fen Road, cross the A10 and take the first turning right, just beyond this junction, onto **Hurst Lane**, again following signs for the Bishop's Way.

To Little Downham

4km

Head past **Pond Farm** and follow the farm track (still Hurst Lane) beyond it for 750m; where the farm track bends to the left, take the grassy, tree-lined drove road (still Hurst Lane), which heads north towards Little Downham. After about 1.5km, the drove road becomes a tarred lane, which runs up into the village. Head straight on at the tiny crossroads, along Chapel Lane, by the eponymous chapel to reach **Main Street**.

Here, bear left then first right along Eagle's Lane, at the end of which you can see the remains of the **Bishop's Palace** across the field from the gate. The estate was established in 970 AD by Athelwold, Bishop of Winchester, later becoming the summer retreat of the bishops of Ely. For a much better view of the palace's remains, carry on down Mary Road and turn right at the T-junction onto Park Plane and down to Tower Farm; most of the palace has long since fallen into disrepair and been demolished, but the two-storey farmhouse is clearly part of the original red-brick structure.

On to Chettisham

4km

Retrace your steps to Main Street, then turn left and follow it through the village, where you'll find *The Plough*, which serves pub **lunches**, and past the village church to reach the village green, where the B1411 heads straight on, back towards Ely. Follow this for 750m, passing the remains of a **windmill** at the junction with Cowbridge Hall Road and turning left at the next junction, **Marshall Lane**. Soon the tarred road gives way to grassy drove roads, ancient tracks through what was originally boggy fen. Head straight on down the first of these tracks and take the right turn a few hundred metres further on, following this drove road south to a T-junction some 300m further on. Turn left onto this grassy track and follow it as it first heads east, then veers round to the north, skirting Chettisham Meadows before depositing you at the busy A10 just outside the village of **Chettisham**. Cross the A10 and head up the track opposite towards the church. Here, the track bears right and leads you onto **The Hamlet**, Chettisham's main road.

Back to the city

6.5km

At the end of The Hamlet, you can turn right onto **Lynn Road**, the main road back into Ely, which heads through farmland directly back to the cathedral (knocking 3.5km off the main route). For a more pleasant, more circuitous return to the city, turn left onto Lynn Road. Just beyond the level crossing, head through the gate to the right and follow **Kettlesworth Drove**, passing deep drainage ditches to meet a path just before the Great Ouse. Turn right and follow this down to a second level crossing over the railway. Cross and continue south along the aptly named **Clayway Drove** – this can be horribly sticky in wet weather – passing paddocks, a small pond and a white water tower to the left before reaching Prickwillow Road (the B1382). Turn right and follow the road uphill, past **Roswell Pits** boating lakes and on to meet Lynn Road just over 1.5km from the end of Clayway Drove. Turn left, passing the cathedral and Palace Green, and continuing on down The Gallery and Back Hill to Station Road and **Ely train station**.

Rough Guides
smooth travel

History · Internet · Music
Restaurants · Football · Formula 1
Weather · Astronomy · Health
Movies · Videogaming · TV

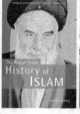

Rough Guides
not just travel